# FINANCIAL PLANNING AND MANAGEMENT

# FINANCIAL PLANNING AND MANAGEMENT

**Anshu Rohtagi**

**CYBER TECH PUBLICATIONS**
4264/3, Ansari Road, Daryaganj, New Delhi-110002 (India)
Ph.: 011-23244078. Fax: 011-23280028
E-Mail: cyberpublicationsdelhi@yahoo.com

# FINANCIAL PLANNING AND MANAGEMENT

**Anshu Rohtagi**



First Edition 2009



*Published by :*

**G.S. Rawat** for **Cyber Tech Publications**
4264/3, Ansari Road, Daryaganj, New Delhi-110002 (India)
Ph.: 011-23244078. Fax: 011-23280028
E-Mail: cyberpublicationsdelhi@yahoo.com

*Printed at :* Asian Offset Printers

# Preface

This book is likely to infuriate some stockbrokers, insurance agents, tax professionals and lawyers. Professional investment managers are likely to dismiss the ideas in this book as being simplistic and as overlooking an assortment of risk management techniques like trailing stop losses, put options and various hedging techniques. However, we did not overlook these portfolio risk management techniques of professional investors. I elected to ignore them and to offer a simpler alternative for the amateur investor.

This book is not only for financial or investment professionals. This book is written for shell shocked individual investors who are more concerned about the safety of their investments than about the correlation of risk and return in the allocation of assets within a portfolio.

I make no pretense that the concepts in this book are original with me. Many other investment advisors have advocated similar concepts to help investors to minimize their losses from various kinds of risk. What is unique about this book is that it integrates a variety of disciplines in a way that can be implemented by individual investors with a minimum of professional help.

This book describes an expanded approach to asset allocation that does not require the use of a computer program to administer. It shows how the combined impact of inflation and taxes can devastate the real rate of return after taxes for conservative investors. It offers a variety of legal ways to minimize taxes in an investment portfolio so as to increase the after tax rate of return without commensurate increases in risk.

Undersigned is confident enough that this book will prove its worth among the general readers and professionals alike. Your valuable suggestions and comments are always welcome.

*—Author*

# CONTENTS

# 1

# INTRODUCTION

Studies overwhelmingly identify bad management as the leading cause of business failure. Bad management translates to poor planning by management.

All too often, the owner is so caught up in the day-to-day tasks of getting the product out the door and struggling to collect receivables to meet the payroll that he or she does not plan. There never seems to be time to prepare Pro Formas or Budgets. Often new managers understand their products but not the financial statements or the bookkeeping records, which they feel are for the benefit of the IRS or the bank.

Such overburdened owner/managers can scarcely identify what will affect their businesses next week, let alone over the coming months and years. But, you may ask, "What should I do? How can I, as a small business owner/manager, avoid getting bogged down? How can I ensure success?"

Success may be ensured only by focusing on all factors affecting a business's performance. Focusing on planning is essential to survival.

Short-term planning is generally concerned with profit planning or budgeting. Long-term planning is generally strategic, setting goals for sales growth and profitability over a minimum of three to five years.

The tools for short- and long-term plans have been explained previously in this section: Pro Forma Income Statements, Cash Flow Statements or Budgets, Ratio Analysis, and pricing considerations. The business's short-term plan should be prepared on a monthly basis for a year into the future, employing the Pro Forma Income Statement and the Cash Flow Budget.

## LONG-TERM PLANNING

The long-term or strategic plan focuses on Pro Forma Statements of Income prepared for annual periods three to five years into the future. You may be asking yourself, "How can I possibly predict what will affect my business that far into the future?" Granted, it's hard to imagine all the variables that will affect your business in the next year, let alone the next three to five years. The key, however, is control - control of your business's future course of expansion through the use of the financial tools explained in this section.

First determine a rate of growth that is desirable and reasonably attainable. Then employ Pro Formas and Cash Flow Budgets to calculate the capital required to finance the inventory, plant, equipment, and personnel needs necessary to attain that growth in sales volume. The business owner/manager must anticipate capital needs in time to make satisfactory arrangements for outside funds if internally generated funds from retained earnings are insufficient.

Growth can be funded in only two ways: with profits or by borrowing. If expansion outstrips the capital available to support higher levels of accounts receivable, inventory, fixed assets, and operating expenses, a business's development will be slowed or stopped entirely by its failure to meet debts as they become payable. Such insolvency will result in the business's assets being liquidated to meet the demands of the creditors. The only way to avoid this "outstripping of capital" is by planning to control growth. Growth must be understood to be controlled. This understanding requires knowledge of past financial performance and of the future requirements of the business.

These needs must be forecast in writing - using the Pro Forma Income Statement in particular - for three to five years in the future. After projecting reasonable sales volumes and profitability, use the Cash Flow Budget to determine (on a quarterly basis for the next three to five years) how these projected sales volumes translate into the flow of cash in and out of the business during normal operations. Where additional inventory, equipment, or other physical assets are necessary to support the sales forecast, you must determine whether or not the business will generate enough profit to sustain the growth forecast.

Often, businesses simply grow too rapidly for internally generated cash to sufficiently support the growth. If profits are inadequate to carry the growth forecast, the owner/manager must either make arrangements for working growth capital to borrowed, or slow growth to allow internal cash to "catch up" and keep pace with the expansion. Because arranging financing and obtaining additional equity capital takes time, this need must be anticipated well in advance to avoid business interruption.

To develop effective long-term plans, you should do the following steps:

1. Determine your personal objectives and how they affect your willingness and ability to pursue financial goals for your business. This consideration, often overlooked, will help you determine whether or not your business goals fit your personal plans. For example, suppose you hope to become a millionaire

by age 45 through your business but your long-term strategic plan reveals that only modest sales growth and very slim profit margins on that volume are attainable in your industry. You must either adjust your personal goals or get into a different business. Long range planning enables you to be realistic about the future of your personal and business expectations.

2. Set goals and objectives for the company (growth rates, return on investment, and direction as the business expands and matures). Express these goals in specific numbers, for example, sales growth of 10 percent a year, increases in gross and net profit margins of 2 to 3 percent a year, a return on investment of not less than 9 to 10 percent a year. Use these long-range plans to develop forecasts of sales and profitability and compare actual results from operations to these forecasts. If after these goals are established actual performance continuously falls short of target, the wise business owner will reassess both the realism of expectations and the desirability of continuing to pursue the enterprise.
3. Develop long-range plans that enable you to attain your goals and objectives. Focus on the strengths and weaknesses of your business and on internal and external factors that will affect the accomplishment of your goals. Develop strategies based upon careful analysis of all relevant factors (pricing strategies, market potential, competition, cost of borrowed and equity capital as compared to using only profits for expansions, etc.) to provide direction for the future of your business.
4. Focus on the financial, human, and physical requirements necessary to fulfill your plan by developing forecasts of sales, expenses, and retain earnings over the next three to five years.

5. Study methods of operation, product mix, new market opportunities, and other such factors to help identify ways to improve your company's productivity and profitability.
6. Revise, revise. Always use your most recent financial statements to adjust your short- and long-term plans. Compare your company's financial performance regularly with current industry data to determine how your results compare with others in your industry. Learn where your business may have performance weaknesses. Don't be afraid to modify your plans if your expectations have been either too aggressive or too conservative.

## CORPORATE FINANCE

Corporate finance is an area of finance dealing with the financial decisions corporations make and the tools and analysis used to make these decisions. The primary goal of corporate finance is to maximize corporate value while reducing the firm's financial risks. Although it is in principle different from managerial finance which studies the financial decisions of all firms, rather than corporations alone, the main concepts in the study of corporate finance are applicable to the financial problems of all kinds of firms.

The discipline can be divided into long-term and short-term decisions and techniques. Capital investment decisions are long-term choices about which projects receive investment, whether to finance that investment with equity or debt, and when or whether to pay dividends to shareholders. On the other hand, the short term decisions can be grouped under the heading "Working capital management". This subject deals with the short-term balance of current assets and current liabilities; the focus here is on managing cash, inventories, and short-term borrowing and lending (such as the terms on credit extended to customers).

The terms Corporate finance and Corporate financier are also associated with investment banking. The typical role of an investment banker is to evaluate investment projects for a bank to make investment decisions.

## Capital Investment Decisions

Capital investment decisions are long-term corporate finance decisions relating to fixed assets and capital structure. Decisions are based on several inter-related criteria. Corporate management seeks to maximize the value of the firm by investing in projects which yield a positive net present value when valued using an appropriate discount rate. These projects must also be financed appropriately. If no such opportunities exist, maximizing shareholder value dictates that management return excess cash to shareholders. Capital investment decisions thus comprise an investment decision, a financing decision, and a dividend decision.

## The Investment Decision

Management must allocate limited resources between competing opportunities ("projects") in a process known as capital budgeting. Making this capital allocation decision requires estimating the value of each opportunity or project: a function of the size, timing and predictability of future cash flows.

## Project Valuation

In general, each project's value will be estimated using a discounted cash flow (DCF) valuation, and the opportunity with the highest value, as measured by the resultant net present value (NPV) will be selected (see Fisher separation theorem). This requires estimating the size and timing of all of the incremental cash flows resulting from the project. These future cash flows are then discounted to determine their *present value* (see Time value of money). These present values are then summed, and this sum net of the initial investment outlay is the NPV.

The NPV is greatly influenced by the discount rate. Thus selecting the proper discount rate—the project "hurdle rate"—is critical to making the right decision. The hurdle rate is the minimum acceptable return on an investment—i.e. the project appropriate discount rate. The hurdle rate should reflect the riskiness of the investment, typically measured by volatility of cash flows, and must take into account the financing mix. Managers use models such as the CAPM or the APT to estimate a discount rate appropriate for a particular project, and use the weighted average cost of capital (*WACC*) to reflect the financing mix selected. (A common error in choosing a discount rate for a project is to apply a WACC that applies to the entire firm. Such an approach may not be appropriate where the risk of a particular project differs markedly from that of the firm's existing portfolio of assets.)

In conjunction with NPV, there are several other measures used as (secondary) selection criteria in corporate finance. These are visible from the DCF and include payback period, IRR, Modified IRR, equivalent annuity, capital efficiency, and ROI.

## VALUING FLEXIBILITY

In many cases, for example R&D projects, a project may open (or close) paths of action to the company, but this reality will not typically be captured in a strict NPV approach. Management will therefore (sometimes) employ tools which place an explicit value on these options. So, whereas in a DCF valuation the most likely or average or scenario specific cash flows are discounted (see John Burr Williams: Theory), here the "flexibile and staged nature" of the investment is modelled, and hence "all" potential payoffs are considered. The difference between the two valuations is the "option value" inherent in the project.

The two most common tools are Decision Tree Analysis (DTA) and Real options analysis:

The DTA approach attempts to capture flexibility by incorporating *likely events* and consequent *management decisions* into the valuation. In the decision tree, each management decision in response to an "event" generates a "branch" or "path" which the company could follow. (For example, management will only proceed with stage 2 of the project given that stage 1 was successful; stage 3, in turn, depends on stage 2. In a DCF model, on the other hand, there is no "branching" - each scenario must be modelled separately.)

The highest value path (probability weighted) is regarded as representative of project value. The real options approach is used when the value of a project is *contingent* on the *value* of some other asset or underlying variable. (For example, the viability of a mining project is contingent on the price of gold; if the price is too low, management will abandon the mining rights, if sufficiently high, management will develop the ore body.

Again, a DCF valuation would capture only one of these outcomes.) Here, using financial option theory as a framework, the decision to be taken is identified as corresponding to either a call option or a put option - valuation is then via the Binomial model or, less often for this purpose, via Black Scholes; see Contingent claim valuation.

The "true" value of the project is then the NPV of the "most likely" scenario plus the option value.

## Quantifying Uncertainty

Given the uncertainty inherent in project forecasting and valuation, analysts will wish to assess the *sensitivity* of project NPV to the various inputs to the DCF model. In a typical sensitivity analysis the analyst will vary one key factor, while *ceteris paribus* holding constant all other inputs. The sensitivity of NPV to a change in that factor is then observed (calculated as " NPV / " factor). For example, the analyst will set annual revenue growth rates at 5% for "Worst Case", 10% for "Likely Case" and 25% for "Best Case" - and produce three corresponding NPVs.

Using a related technique, analysts may also run scenario based forecasts so as to observe the value of the project under various outcomes. Under this technique, a scenario comprises a particular outcome for economy-wide, "global" factors (exchange rates, commodity prices) *as well as* for company-specific factors (revenue growth rates, unit costs). Analysts may also plot these results to produce a "value-surface" (or even a "value-space"), where NPV is a function of several variables. Here, extending the analysis, key inputs in addition to growth are also adjusted, and NPV is calculated for the various scenarios.

A further advancement is to construct stochastic or probabilistic financial models (as opposed to the traditional static and deterministic models). For this purpose, the most common method is to use Monte Carlo simulation to analyze the project's NPV. Here, the cash flow components that are (heavily) impacted by uncertainty are simulated, mathematically reflecting their "random characteristics". The simulation produces several *thousand* trials (in contrast to the scenario approach above) and outputs a histogram of project NPV. The average NPV of the potential investment - as well as its volatility and other sensitivities - is then observed. (Typically, an add-in such as Crystal Ball is used to run simulations in spreadsheet based DCF models.)

Here, continuing the above example, instead of assigning three discrete values to revenue growth, the analyst would assign an appropriate probability distribution (commonly the triangular distribution). This distribution - and that of the other sources of uncertainty - would then be "sampled" repeatedly so as to generate the several thousand realistic (but random) scenarios, and the output is a realistic, representative set of valuations. The resultant statistics (average NPV and standard deviation of NPV) will be a more accurate mirror of the project's "randomness" than the variance observed under the traditional scenario based approach.

## The Financing Decision

Achieving the goals of corporate finance requires that any corporate investment be financed appropriately. As above, since both hurdle rate and cash flows (and hence the riskiness of the firm) will be affected, the financing mix can impact the valuation. Management must therefore identify the "optimal mix" of financing—the capital structure that results in maximum value. (See Balance sheet, WACC, Fisher separation theorem; but, see also the Modigliani-Miller theorem.)

The sources of financing will, generically, comprise some combination of debt and equity. Financing a project through debt results in a liability that must be serviced—and hence there are cash flow implications regardless of the project's success. Equity financing is less risky in the sense of cash flow commitments, but results in a dilution of ownership and earnings. The *cost of equity* is also typically higher than the *cost of debt* (see CAPM and WACC), and so equity financing may result in an increased hurdle rate which may offset any reduction in cash flow risk.

Management must also attempt to match the financing mix to the asset being financed as closely as possible, in terms of both timing and cash flows.

One of the main theories of how firms make their financing decisions is the Pecking Order Theory, which suggests that firms avoid external financing while they have internal financing available and avoid new equity financing while they can engage in new debt financing at reasonably low interest rates. Another major theory is the Trade-Off Theory in which firms are assumed to trade-off the Tax Benefits of debt with the Bankruptcy Costs of debt when making their decisions.

An emerging area in finance theory is Right-financing whereby investment banks and corporations can enhance investment return and company value over time by determining the right investment objectives, policy framework, institutional structure, source of financing (debt or equity) and expenditure framework within a given economy and under given market conditions. One last theory about this decision is the Market timing hypothesis which states that firms look for the cheaper type of financing regardless of their current levels of internal resources, debt and equity.

## The Dividend Decision

In general, management must decide whether to invest in additional projects, reinvest in existing operations, or return free cash as dividends to shareholders. The dividend is calculated mainly on the basis of the company's unappropriated profit and its business prospects for the coming year. If there are no NPV positive opportunities, i.e. where returns exceed the hurdle rate, then management must return excess cash to investors. These *free cash flows* comprise cash remaining after all business expenses have been met.

This is the general case, however there are exceptions. For example, investors in a "Growth stock", expect that the company will, almost by definition, retain earnings so as to fund growth internally. In other cases, even though an opportunity is currently NPV negative, management may consider "investment flexibility" / potential payoffs and decide to retain cash flows; see above and Real options.

Management must also decide on the form of the distribution, generally as cash dividends or via a share buyback. There are various considerations: where shareholders pay tax on dividends, companies may elect to retain earnings, or to perform a stock buyback, in both cases increasing the value of shares outstanding; some companies will pay "dividends" from stock rather than in cash. Today it is generally accepted that dividend policy is value neutral seeModigliani-Miller theorem).

## Working Capital Management

Decisions relating to working capital and short term financing are referred to as *working capital management.* These involve managing the relationship between a firm's short-term assets and its short-term liabilities. The goal of Working capital management is to ensure that the firm is able to continue its operations and that it has sufficient cash flow to satisfy both maturing short-term debt and upcoming operational expenses.

## Decision Criteria

By definition, Working capital management entails short term decisions - generally, relating to the next one year period - which are "reversible". These decisions are therefore not taken on the same basis as Capital Investment Decisions (NPV or related, as above) rather they will be based on cash flows and/ or profitability.

- One measure of cash flow is provided by the cash conversion cycle - the net number of days from the outlay of cash for raw material to receiving payment from the customer. As a management tool, this metric makes explicit the inter-relatedness of decisions relating to inventories, accounts receivable and payable, and cash. Because this number effectively corresponds to the time that the firm's cash is tied up in operations and unavailable for other activities, management generally aims at a low net count.

In this context, the most useful measure of profitability is Return on capital (ROC). The result is shown as a percentage, determined by dividing relevant income for the 12 months by capital employed; Return on equity (ROE) shows this result for the firm's shareholders. Firm value is enhanced when, and if, the return on capital, which results from working capital management, exceeds the cost of capital, which results from capital investment decisions as above. ROC measures are therefore useful as a management tool, in that they link short-term policy with long-term decision making. See Economic value added (EVA).

## Management of working capital

Guided by the above criteria, management will use a combination of policies and techniques for the management of working capital. These policies aim at managing the *current assets* (generally cash and cash equivalents, inventories and debtors) and the short term financing, such that cash flows and returns are acceptable.

- Cash management. Identify the cash balance which allows for the business to meet day to day expenses, but reduces cash holding costs.
- Inventory management. Identify the level of inventory which allows for uninterrupted production but

reduces the investment in raw materials - and minimizes reordering costs - and hence increases cash flow; see Supply chain management; Just In Time (JIT); Economic order quantity (EOQ); Economic production quantity (EPQ).

- Debtors management. Identify the appropriate credit policy, i.e. credit terms which will attract customers, such that any impact on cash flows and the cash conversion cycle will be offset by increased revenue and hence Return on Capital (or *vice versa*); see Discounts and allowances.
- Short term financing. Identify the appropriate source of financing, given the cash conversion cycle: the inventory is ideally financed by credit granted by the supplier; however, it may be necessary to utilize a bank loan (or overdraft), or to "convert debtors to cash" through "factoring".

## FINANCIAL RISK MANAGEMENT

Risk management is the process of measuring risk and then developing and implementing strategies to manage that risk. Financial risk management focuses on risks that can be managed ("hedged") using traded financial instruments (typically changes in commodity prices, interest rates, foreign exchange rates and stock prices). Financial risk management will also play an important role in cash management.

This area is related to corporate finance in two ways. Firstly, firm exposure to business risk is a direct result of previous Investment and Financing decisions. Secondly, both disciplines share the goal of creating, or enhancing, firm value. All large corporations have risk management teams, and small firms practice informal, if not formal, risk management.

Derivatives are the instruments most commonly used in Financial risk management. Because unique derivative contracts tend to be costly to create and monitor, the most cost-effective financial risk management methods usually involve derivatives that trade on well-established financial markets. These standard derivative instruments include options, futures contracts, forward contracts, and swaps.

## Relationship with Other Areas in Finance

### *Investment Banking*

Use of the term "corporate finance" varies considerably across the world. In the United States it is used, as above, to describe activities, decisions and techniques that deal with many aspects of a company's finances and capital. In the United Kingdom and Commonwealth countries, the terms "corporate finance" and "corporate financier" tend to be associated with investment banking - i.e. with transactions in which capital is raised for the corporation.

### Personal and Public Finance

Corporate finance utilizes tools from almost all areas of finance. Some of the tools developed by and for corporations have broad application to entities other than corporations, for example, to partnerships, sole proprietorships, not-for-profit organizations, governments, mutual funds, and personal wealth management. But in other cases their application is very limited outside of the corporate finance arena. Because corporations deal in quantities of money much greater than individuals, the analysis has developed into a discipline of its own. It can be differentiated from personal finance and public finance.

# 2

# CAPITAL BUDGETING

Capital budgeting (or investment appraisal) is the planning process used to determine a firm's long term investments such as new machinery, replacement machinery, new plants, new products, and research and development projects.

Many formal methods are used in capital budgeting, including the techniques such as:

- Net present value
- Profitability index
- Internal rate of return
- Modified Internal Rate of Return, and
- Equivalent annuity.

These methods use the incremental cash flows from each potential investment, or *project*. Techniques based on accounting earnings and accounting rules are sometimes used - though economists consider this to be improper - such as the *accounting rate of return,* and "return on investment." Simplified and hybrid methods are used as well, such as *payback period* and *discounted payback period.*

## NET PRESENT VALUE

Each potential project's value should be estimated using a discounted cash flow (DCF) valuation, to find its net present value (NPV) - (see Fisher separation theorem). This valuation requires estimating the size and timing of all of the incremental cash flows from the project. These future cash flows are then discounted to determine their *present value*. These present values are then summed, to get the NPV. See also Time value of money. The NPV decision rule is to accept all positive NPV projects in an unconstrained environment, or if projects are mutually exclusive, accept the one with the highest NPV.

The NPV is greatly affected by the discount rate, so selecting the proper rate - sometimes called the *hurdle rate* - is critical to making the right decision. The hurdle rate is the minimum acceptable return on an investment. It should reflect the riskiness of the investment, typically measured by the volatility of cash flows, and must take into account the financing mix. Managers may use models such as the CAPM or the APT to estimate a discount rate appropriate for each particular project, and use the weighted average cost of capital (*WACC*) to reflect the financing mix selected. A common practice in choosing a discount rate for a project is to apply a WACC that applies to the entire firm, but a higher discount rate may be more appropriate when a project's risk is higher than the risk of the firm as a whole.

## INTERNAL RATE OF RETURN

The internal rate of return (IRR) is defined as the discount rate that gives a net present value (NPV) of zero. It is a commonly used measure of investment efficiency.

The IRR method will result in the same decision as the NPV method for independent (non-mutually exclusive) projects in an unconstrained environment, in the usual cases where a negative cash flow occurs at the start of the project, followed by all positive cash flows. In most realistic cases, all independent projects that have an IRR higher than the hurdle rate should be accepted. Nevertheless, for mutually exclusive projects, the decision rule of taking the project with the highest IRR - which is often used - may select a project with a lower NPV.

In some cases, several zero NPV discount rates may exist, so there is no unique IRR. The IRR exists and is unique if one or more years of net investment (negative cash flow) are followed by years of net revenues. But if the signs of the cash flows change more than once, there may be several IRRs. The IRR equation generally cannot be solved analytically but only via iterations.

One shortcoming of the IRR method is that it is commonly misunderstood to convey the actual annual profitability of an investment. However, this is not the case because intermediate cash flows are almost never reinvested at the project's IRR; and, therefore, the actual rate of return is almost certainly going to be lower. Accordingly, a measure called Modified Internal Rate of Return (MIRR) is often used.

Despite a strong academic preference for NPV, surveys indicate that executives prefer IRR over NPV, although they should be used in concert. In a budget-constrained environment, efficiency measures should be used to maximize the overall NPV of the firm. Some managers find it intuitively more appealing to evaluate investments in terms of percentage rates of return than dollars of NPV.

### Equivalent Annuity Method

The *equivalent annuity* method expresses the NPV as an annualized cash flow by dividing it by the present value of the annuity factor. It is often used when assessing only the costs of specific projects that have the same cash inflows. In this form it is known as the *equivalent annual cost* (EAC) method and is the cost per year of owning and operating an asset over its entire lifespan. It is often used when comparing investment projects of unequal lifespans. For example if project A has an expected lifetime of 7 years, and project B has an expected lifetime of 11 years it would be improper to simply compare the net present values (NPVs) of the two projects, unless the projects could not be repeated.

The use of the EAC method implies that the project will be replaced by an identical project.

Alternatively the *chain method* can be used with the NPV method under the assumption that the projects will be replaced with the same cash flows each time. To compare projects of unequal length, say 3 years and 4 years, the projects are *chained together*, i.e. four repetitions of the 3 year project are compare to three repetitions of the 4 year project. The chain method and the EAC method give mathematically equivalent answers.

The assumption of the same cash flows for each link in the chain is essentially an assumption of zero inflation, so a real interest rate rather than a nominal interest rate is commonly used in the calculations.

## Real Options

Real options analysis has become important since the 1970s as option pricing models have gotten more sophisticated. The discounted cash flow methods essentially value projects as if they were risky bonds, with the promised cash flows known. But managers will have many choices of how to increase future cash inflows, or to increase future cash outflows.

In other words, managers get to manage the projects - not simply accept or reject them. Real options analysis try to value the choices - the option value - that the managers will have in the future and adds these values to the NPV.

### Ranked Projects

The real value of capital budgeting is to rank projects. Most organizations have many projects that could potentially be financially rewarding. Once it has been determined that a particular project has exceeded its hurdle, then it should be ranked against peer projects (e.g. - highest IRR to lowest IRR). The highest ranking projects should be implemented until the budgeted capital has been expended.

## CAPITAL BUDGETING TECHNIQUES

A variety of measures have evolved over time to analyze capital budgeting requests. The newer methods use *time value of money* concepts. Older methods, like the payback period, have the deficiency of not using time value techniques and will eventually fall by the wayside and be replaced in companies by the newer, superior methods of evaluation.

The newer methods have one thing in common: they conduct a test to see if the benefits (i.e., cash inflows) are large enough to repay the company for three things:

(1) the cost of the asset,

(2) the cost of financing the asset (e.g., interest), and

(3) a rate of return (called a *risk premium*) that compensates the company for potential errors made when estimating cash flows that will occur in the distant future.

Let's take a look at the most popular techniques for analyzing a capital budgeting proposal.

### Net Present Value (NPV)

Using the hurdle rate as the required rate of return, the *net present value* of an investment is the *present value of the cash inflows* minus the *present value of the cash outflows.* A more common way of expressing this is to say that the net present value (NPV) is the present value of the benefits (PVB) minus the present value of the costs (PVC)

NPV = PVB - PVC

By using the hurdle rate as the discount rate, we are conducting a test to see if the project is expected to earn our minimum desired rate of return. Here are our decision rules:

| **If the NPV is:** | **Benefits vs. Costs** | **Should we expect to earn at least our minimum rate of return?** | **Accept the investment?** |
|---|---|---|---|
| Positive | Benefits > Costs | Yes, more than | Accept |
| Zero | Benefits = Costs | Exactly equal to | Indifferent |
| Negative | Benefits < Costs | No, less than | Reject |

Very important: Notice that, if the NPV is positive, it says that the company expects to receive benefits that are large enough to repay the company for (1) the asset's cost, (2) the cost of financing the project, and (3) a rate of return that adequately compensates the company for the risk found in the cash flow estimates. If the NPV is negative, the benefits are not large enough to cover all three of the above, and therefore the project should be rejected.

## Internal Rate of Return (IRR)

The *Internal Rate of Return (IRR)* is the discount rate that will cause the present value of the benefits to equal the present value of the cost. In other words, the IRR is the situation described in the middle line of the above table. We use a trial-and-error process to find this percentage rate. We generally start by conducting a test using the hurdle rate. This will tell us whether the project is expected to earn us more than or less than the hurdle rate.

| **Test Results** | **Interpretation of Results** | **Next percentage to be tested?** |
|---|---|---|
| PVB > PVC | The project is expected to earn **more** than the percentage rate used for the test | A higher rate |
| PVB < PVC | The project is expected to earn **less** than the percentage rate used for the test | A lower rate |

It isn't necessary to test in increments of one percent (e.g., 10%, 11%, 12%, etc.). Once you have conducted the test using the hurdle rate, compare the PVB and PVC. If the two numbers are relatively close to one another, the IRR is relatively close to the hurdle rate. If the PVB is well away from the PVC, you will need to choose a percentage rate that is well away from the hurdle rate for your second test.

We continue the testing until we find a range of values for the IRR. In other words, we need to know that the IRR is *greater than* some percentage number and *less than* some percentage number (e.g., greater than 10% and less than 15%).

In the interest of accuracy, keep this range to 5% or less, e.g., greater than 12% and less than 13% is ideal, greater than 10% and less than 15% is O.K., greater than 10% and less than 20% is not acceptable for the range. We then set up a proportion and interpolate to find the IRR.

## CALCULATION OF THE IRR

Assume that we are evaluating a project that has a cost of $100,000. Using the hurdle rate, we obtain a PVB of $103,000. Comparing the PVB of $103,000 to the PVC of $3,000, this tells us that the project is expected to earn a rate higher than 10%. So we choose a higher rate for our second test. Since the gap between $103,000 and $100,000 is small (in relative terms), we shouldn't have to go far.

Let's choose 15% for our second test. Using this as our discount rate, we obtain a PVB of $98,000. Since the PVB is now less than the PVC, the IRR is less than 15%. We now have our range: the IRR is between 10% and 15%.

We are searching for the discount rate that will cause the PVB to equal the PVC. Here is what we know so far:

| Percentage Tested | PVB |
|---|---|
| 10% | \$103,000 |
| IRR | \$100,000 |
| 15% | \$ 98,000 |

Notice that we place the smaller percentage number on top (to simplify the arithmetic later). On the middle row, the IRR is the discount rate that will give us a PVB exactly equal to the PVC of \$100,000.

Let's call the distance between 10% and the IRR (above) a distance of $x$. The ratio of this distance to the distance between the outside two numbers (i.e., 10% and 15%) should be the same for both columns. In other words, we can set up a proportion using this: the ratio of the difference between the top two numbers and the outside two numbers is the same for both columns. That is: x is to 5% as \$3,000 is to \$5,000.

$$x \,/\, 5\% = \$3{,}000 \,/\, \$5{,}000$$

$$x = \$3{,}000 \,/\, \$5{,}000 \; * \; 5\%$$

$$x = 0.60 * 5\%$$

$$x = 3.0\%$$

If x is 3.0%, then the IRR is 3% away from 10% and is larger than 10% (since we know that the IRR is between 10% and 15%); therefore, the IRR must be 13.0%.

## Which Method Is Better: the NPV or the IRR?

Surveys show that the IRR method is the more popular of the two methods (by a small margin). However, the NPV is superior to IRR for at least two reasons:

The NPV assumes that the cash inflows are reinvested to earn the hurdle rate; the IRR assumes that the cash inflows are reinvested to earn the IRR. Of the two, the

NPV's assumption is more realistic in most situations. It is possible for the IRR to have more than one solution. If the cash flows experience a sign change (e.g., positive cash flow in one year, negative in the next), the IRR method will have more than one solution.

In other words, there will be more than one percentage number that will cause the PVB to equal the PVC. (When this occurs, we simply don't use the IRR method to evaluate the project, since no one value of the IRR is theoretically superior to the others.) The NPV method does not have this problem.

## Modified Internal Rate of Return (MIRR)

The *Modified Internal Rate of Return (MIRR)* is an attempt to overcome the above two deficiencies in the IRR method. The cash inflows (which are received at the end of each year) are assumed to be reinvested at the hurdle rate for the remainder of the project's life.

Using the hurdle rate, the MIRR technique calculates the present value of the cash outflows (i.e., the PVC), the future value of the cash inflows (to the end of the project's life), and then solves for the discount rate that will equate the PVC and the future value of the benefits. In this way, the two problems mentioned previously are overcome:

1. the cash inflows are assumed to be reinvested at the firm's hurdle rate, and
2. there is only one solution to the technique.

## Calculation of the MIRR

Assume that we are evaluating a project that has a cost of $30,000, after-tax cash inflows of $10,000 per year for four years, and a hurdle rate of 10%.

Since the cash inflows are assumed to be received at the end of each year, the cash inflows would be reinvested as shown below. Notice that the 1st year's cash inflow is assumed to be reinvested for 3 years, so we multiply it times the future value factor for 10% and year 3 (i.e., 1.331). The 2nd year's cash inflow is assumed to be reinvested for 2 years, so we multiply it time the future value factor for 10% and year 2 (i.e., 1.210).

Year 3's cash inflow is invested for 1 year and year 4's cash inflow is received at the end of the 4th year, so it is not available for reinvestment since it coincides with the end of the project's life.

| Year | Years Reinvested | Cash Inflow | Future Value Factor (at 10%) | Future Value |
|---|---|---|---|---|
| 1 | 3 | $10,000 | 1.331 | $13,310 |
| 2 | 2 | $10,000 | 1.210 | $12,100 |
| 3 | 1 | $10,000 | 1.100 | $11,000 |
| 4 | 0 | $10,000 | 1.000 | $10,000 |
| Total | | | | $46,410 |

Now, the only question remaining is: If I invest $30,000 in an account today and receive the equivalent of $46,410 in four years, what rate would be earned on the investment? We can find the MIRR in one of two ways:

1. The trial-and-error technique that was used earlier to find the IRR. Using any discount rate, like 10%, take the present value of the $46,410 received four years from now. (This is $31,699.) Since the present value of the benefits ($31,699) is larger than the present value of the cost ($30,000), we need to use a higher discount rate, like 12%. At 12%, the present value is $29,494. Since the PVB is now less than the PVC, the MIRR is less than 12%. We now have our range: the MIRR is between 10% and 12%.

We are searching for the discount rate that will cause the PVB to equal the PVC. Here is what we know so far:

| Percentage Tested | PVB |
|---|---|
| 10% | $31,699 |
| MIRR | $30,000 |
| 12% | $29,494 |

On the middle row, the MIRR is the discount rate that will give us a PVB equal to the PVC of $30,000.

Let's call the distance between 10% and the MIRR (above) a distance of *x*. The ratio of this distance to the distance between the outside two numbers (i.e., 10% and 12%) should be the same for both columns. In other words,

$$x / 2\% = \$1,699 / \$2,205$$

$$x = \$1,699 / \$2,205 * 2\%$$

$$x = 0.7705 * 2\%$$

$$x = 1.54\%$$

If x is 1.54%, then the MIRR is 1.54% away from 10% and is larger than 10% (since we know that the MIRR is between 10% and 12%); therefore, the MIRR must be 11.54%.

2. As an easier alternate method, we can solve for the *geometric mean return.*
   a. Divide the future value by the present value (i.e., $46,410/$30,000) to get a value of 1.547. Notice that this is the value that $1.00 would grow to in 4 years if invested at the hurdle rate of 10%.
   b. Set the result to the 1/n power (where n = 4 years). If you have a y-to-the-x key on your calculator, simply enter 1.547 as the y-value and 0.25 (i.e., 1/4) as the x-value, and solve. The result is 1.1153.
   c. Subtract 1.0 from the answer and place the answer (0.1153) in percentage form. The answer is the MIRR of 11.53%.

## Payback Period

The Payback Period is the weakest of the capital budgeting methods discussed here. By definition, the payback period is the length of time that it takes to recover your investment. The payback period of the illustration immediately above is 3.0 years. (To recover $30,000 at the rate of $10,000 per year would take 3.0 years.)

## Other Issues

1. Sunk Costs - Costs that have been incurred in the past and cannot be recovered are not relevant to the analysis. These costs are called *sunk costs.* The only cash flows that matter are those that will change if we decide to accept the project. These cash flows are called *incremental cash flows* (or *relevant cash flows*).
2. Inflation - With the passage of time, inflation will have an impact on the cash flows (e.g., wage rates will likely increase in the future as a result of inflation). *Should the cash flows be adjusted for the impact of inflation?* The answer is: *You have to be consistent in the relationship between the discount rate and the cash flows.*
   a. If the discount rate includes an inflation premium (as it almost always will), then the cash flows should reflect the impact of inflation as well.
   b. If the cash flows do not include the impact of inflation, then the inflation rate should be deducted from the discount rate.

   Follow this link for a more complete examination of how to treat inflation.
3. Scale Effect - If we are considering *mutually exclusive proposals* and the assets (e.g., machines) cost different amounts, there is a potential bias in favor of accepting

the more expensive asset, simply because of the larger size of the price tag. For example, we may consider investing in either:

- Asset A, which cost \$100,000 and has an NPV of \$3,000, or
- Asset B, which cost \$300,000 and has an NPV of \$3,100.

If we make our decision based solely on the NPV's dollar amount, we would choose asset B since it has the higher NPV. However, per dollar invested, asset A obviously has the higher return. If the cost of the two assets differ by a considerable amount, we should use the *profitability index* instead of the NPV to make our decision.

The profitability index, by definition, is the ratio of the present value of the benefits (PVB) to the present value of the cost (PVC). This will remove the scale effect's bias. We obviously prefer the asset that has the higher value for the profitability index.

4. Unequal Lives - If we are comparing mutually exclusive proposals and the assets (e.g., machines) have different lives, there is a bias in favor of accepting the longer-lived asset. To see how to eliminate this bias, read this coverage of replacement chains.

## CAPITAL BUDGETING

### Shenandoah Furniture, Inc.

Shenandoah Furniture is considering replacing one of the machines in its manufacturing facility. The cost of the new machine will be \$76,120. Transportation will cost an additional \$2,500 and the new machine will increase the need for working capital by \$1,400.

The new asset will be depreciated using the MACRS technique over a 5 year period. The company expects to dispose of the machine in 6 years. The expected salvage value for the machine at that time is $2,300.

The savings (before depreciation and taxes) that are associated with the new and old machines are expected to be as follows:

New Asset Old Asset

Year 1 $28,000 Year 1 $2,000

Year 2 25,000 Year 2 2,000

Year 3 19,000 Year 3 2,000

Year 4 16,000 Year 4 2,000

Year 5 14,000 Year 5 2,000

Year 6 5,000 Year 6 2,000

The old machine (the one being replaced) is now 4 years old and can be sold today for $14,300. When originally purchased, this machine cost $54,600. If kept, the scrap value of the old machine will be zero in 6 more years. The accumulated depreciation on the old asset is currently $45,154. (The depreciable life for the machine is the same as for the new machine: five years.)

The hurdle rate for the company is 12%. The firm is in the 34% tax bracket.

Using the various evaluation methods for capital budgeting (e.g. net present value method and the internal rate of return method), determine whether or not the firm should purchase the new asset.

## Solution To Shenandoah Furniture

### *Capital Budgeting Problem*

Since depreciation is a tax deductible item, it affects the amount of the savings that we get to keep (after the government takes its cut). So we first need to calculate what the change in depreciation will be if we decide to buy the new equipment.

Depreciation on the New Asset

(Depreciable Cost = $78,620)

MACRS

*Value: Depreciation*:

Year 1 0.200 Year 1 $15,724

Year 2 0.320 Year 2 25,158

Year 3 0.192 Year 3 15,095

Year 4 0.115 Year 4 9,041

Year 5 0.115 Year 5 9,041

Year 6 0.058 Year 6 4,560

Unused Depreciation on the Old Asset:

(Depreciable Cost = $54,600)

MACRS

*Value Depreciation*:

Year 1 0.000 Year 1 0

Year 2 0.000 Year 2 0

Year 3 0.000 Year 3 0

Year 4 0.000 Year 4 0

Year 5 0.115 Year 5 6,279

Year 6 0.058 Year 6 3,167

Calculation of the Change in Depreciation

(Needed For Determination of Cash Inflows)

New - Old = Increase

Next Year = $15,724 - $6,279 = $9,445

Year 2 = 25,158 - 3,167 = 21,992

Year 3 = 15,095 - 0 = 15,095

Year 4 = 9,041 - 0 = 9,041

Year 5 = 9,041 - 0 = 9,041

Year 6 = 4,560 - 0 = 4,560

Determination of Cash Inflows

Now that we know the change in depreciation, we can calculate the amount of money that the company will get to keep from its net savings (i.e., the cash inflow for each year).

Yr. Net Savings x (1-t.r.) +

Chg. in

Deprec. x

Tax

Rate = Cash Inflow*

1 26,000 x 0.66 + 9,445 x 0.34 = $20,371

2 23,000 x 0.66 + 21,992 x 0.34 = 22,657

3 17,000 x 0.66 + 15,095 x 0.34 = 16,352

4 14,000 x 0.66 + 9,041 x 0.34 = 12,314

5 12,000 x 0.66 + 9,041 x 0.34 = 10,994

6 3,000 x 0.66 + 4,560 x 0.34 = 3,530

* Does Not Include These Terminal Cash Flows:

Working Capital = $1,400 (Cash Inflow)

+ Salvage Value = 2,300 (Cash Inflow)

- Tax on Salvage Value = 782 (Cash Outflow)

Total Terminal Cash Flows = $2,918 (Cash Inflow)

### *Net Present Value of the Project*

We are now ready to test whether the equipment will be profitable for us (i.e., whether it will return our investment, our financing cost, and a profit large enough to compensate us for accepting the risk in the project).

CASH OUTFLOWS @ 12% CASH INFLOWS

(0) Cost of Asset $76,120 (1) $20,371 x 0.893 = $18,192

Transportation 2,500 (2) 22,657 x 0.797 = 18,058

Working Capital 1,400 (3) 16,352 x 0.712 = 11,643

Sale Proceeds (14,300) (4) 12,314 x 0.636 = 7,832

Tax on Sale of Old 1,650 (5) 10,994 x 0.567 = 6,234

(6) 6,448 x 0.507 = 3,269

*P.V. of Costs* = $67,370 *P.V. of Benefits* = $65,227

Net Present Value = ($2,143)

where the tax on the sale of the old asset is:

*Step #1:* Original Cost $54,600 *Step #2:* Selling Price $14,300- Accum. Deprec. - 45,154 - Book Value - 9,446

Book Value $ 9,446 Gain (Loss) $4,854

*Step #3:* Gain (or Loss) $4,854

x Tax Rate x 0.34

Tax on Sale of Old Asset $1,650

Internal Rate of Return (IRR)

Now for the profitability expressed as a percent (rather than in dollars) – the internal rate of return:

10% 68,388

X

(difference on top)

1,017

(difference on top)

1%

(outside difference)

I.R.R. 67,370 1,598

(outside difference)

11% 66,790

X

1% = 1,017

1,598

X = 1,017

1,598

* 1%

X = 0.64%

The I.R.R. is 10.64%.

Modified internal rate of return (MIRR)

CASH OUTFLOWS @ 12% CASH INFLOWS

(0) Cost of Asset $76,120 (1) $20,371 x 1.762 = $35,901

Transportation 2,500 (2) 22,657 x 1.574 = 35,651

Working Capital 1,400 (3) 16,352 x 1.405 = 22,974

Sale Proceeds (14,300) (4) 12,314 x 1.254 = 15,447

Tax on Sale of Old 1,650 (5) 10,994 x 1.120 = 12,313

(6) 6,448 x 1.000 = 6,448

*P.V. of Costs* = $67,370 *F.V. of Benefits* = $128,735

If the project costs $67,370 today and it generates cash of $128,735 after six years, what is the project's rate of return? We use the geometric mean return formula to solve for the rate of return:

Rate of return 0.1140 or11.40%

Rate of return 1.9109 -1

Rate of return 1.9109 -1

-1

$67,370

Rate of return $128,735

-1

Beginning value

Ending value

Rate of return

0.166667

)61(6

n

## SUMMARY OF CAPITAL BUDGETING MEASURES

***Method Conclusion***

Net Present Value = ($2,143) Reject the project: negative NPV

Profitability Index = 0.97 Reject the project: less than 1.00

Modified IRR = 11.40% Reject the project: less than hurdle rate

Internal Rate of Return = 10.64% Reject the project: less than hurdle rate

Payback Period (years) = 3.65 Reject if required payback is <3.65 years

## CAPITAL BUDGETING

### Seal-A-Deal, Inc.

Seal-A-Deal, Inc. is a company that specializes in negotiating contracts for professional athletes.

The company handles labor contracts, deals involving advertising products, appearances at special events, and other types of contracts. The firm is considering the purchase of a new highspeed Xerox machine, which will make its operations more efficient.

As one of the financial managers of Seal-A-Deal, you have determined that the best machine for the job is a Xerox 3600 machine. The new machine will cost $43,588, require transportation of $800, and will also require $1,412 in working capital to support the new machine's operations.

The machine will be depreciated over a 5-year period and will have a salvage value of $1,315 at the end of the expected economic life of six years. The company will not deduct the salvage value when calculating depreciation.

The new machine will replace an old Xerox machine that has seen its better days. The maintenance savings are expected to be as follows:

Year Number 1 $8,100

Year Number 2 7,800

Year Number 3 7,400

Year Number 4 7,000

Year Number 5 6,550

Year Number 6 6,200

The old machine can be sold for $8,300. It is now three years old and originally cost $36,000.

The firm has a hurdle rate of 6% for all potential projects and has a marginal tax rate of 34%.

a. Determine the depreciation associated with the new machine, for each year.

Depreciation on New Asset

(Depreciable Cost = $44,388)

| MACRS | Value | | Depreciation |
|---|---|---|---|
| Year 1 | 0.200 | Year 1 | $8,878 |
| Year 2 | 0.320 | Year 2 | 14,204 |
| Year 3 | 0.192 | Year 3 | 8,522 |
| Year 4 | 0.115 | Year 4 | 5,105 |
| Year 5 | 0.115 | Year 5 | 5,105 |
| Year 6 | 0.058 | Year 6 | 2,575 |

b. Determine the unused depreciation on the old machine.

Unused Depreciation on Old Asset

(Depreciable Cost = $36,000)

| MACRS | Value | | Depreciation |
|---|---|---|---|
| Year 1 | 0.000 | Year 1 | 0 |
| Year 2 | 0.000 | Year 2 | 0 |
| Year 3 | 0.000 | Year 3 | 0 |
| Year 4 | 0.115 | Year 4 | 4,140 |
| Year 5 | 0.115 | Year 5 | 4,140 |
| Year 6 | 0.058 | Year 6 | 2,088 |

*Note:* The accumulated depreciation for the first three years is not shown here but is equal to $25,632. In other words, the accumulated depreciation is equal to the sum of the first three values in the MACRS table times the depreciable cost: i.e.

(0.200 + 0.320 + 0.192) * $36,000 = $25,632.

c. Determine the cash inflows (after depreciation and taxes) associated with the new machine.

***Calculation of Change in Depreciation***

(needed for the calculation of the cash inflows)

New - Old = Increase

Next Year = $8,878 - $4,140 = $4,738

Year 2 = 14,204 - 4,140 = 10,064

Year 3 = 8,522 - 2,088 = 6,434

Year 4 = 5,105 - 0 = 5,105

Year 5 = 5,105 - 0 = 5,105

Year 6 = 2,575 - 0 = 2,575

***Determination of Cash Inflows***

Yr. Net Savings x (1-t.r.) +

Chg. in

Deprec. x

Tax

Rate = Cash Inflow*

1 8,100 x 0.66 + 4,738 x 0.34 = $6,957

2 7,800 x 0.66 + 10,064 x 0.34 = 8,570

3 7,400 x 0.66 + 6,434 x 0.34 = 7,072

4 7,000 x 0.66 + 5,105 x 0.34 = 6,356

5 6,550 x 0.66 + 5,105 x 0.34 = 6,059

6 6,200 x 0.66 + 2,575 x 0.34 = 4,967

* Does Not Include These Terminal Cash Flows:

Working Capital = $1,412 (Cash Inflow)

Change in Salvage Value = 1,315 (Cash Inflow)

Tax on Salvage Value = 447 (Cash Outflow)

Total Terminal Cash Flows = $2,280 (Cash Inflow) where the tax on the salvage value of the new asset (shown above) is:

Salvage Value $1,315 x Tax Rate x 0.34

Tax on Sale of New Asset $ 447

d. Determine the cash outflows associated with the machine. Then determine the present value of both the cash outflows and the cash inflows.

CASH OUTFLOWS @ 6% CASH INFLOWS

(0) Cost of Asset 43,588 (1) 6,957 x 0.943 = $6,560

Transportation 800 (2) 8,570 x 0.890 = 7,627

Working Capital 1,412 (3) 7,072 x 0.840 = 5,940

Sale Proceeds (8,300) (4) 6,356 x 0.792 = 5,034

Tax on Sale of Old (703) (5) 6,059 x 0.747 = 4,526

(6) 7,247 x 0.705 = 5,109

*P.V. of Costs* = $36,797 *P.V. of Benefits* = $34,796

where the Tax on the Sale of the Old Asset is:

*Step #1:* Original Cost $36,000 *Step #2:* Selling Price $8,300

- Accum. Deprec. - 25,632 - Book Value 10,362

Book Value $10,368 Gain (Loss) ($2,068)

*Step #3:* Gain (or Loss) ($2,068)

x Tax Rate x 0.34

Tax on Sale of Old Asset ($ 703)

Determine the net present value of the proposed project, as well as the profitability index.

By definition, the Net Present Value is equal to the Present Value of the Benefits minus the Present Value of the Costs. Therefore, the Net Present Value is $34,796 - $36,797 or an NPV of ($2,001).

The Profitability Index is a ratio of the benefits to the costs. Therefore, the Profitability Index is 0.95 for this project. Determine the internal rate of return on the new machine. When we used 6% as the discount rate, we found that the project has a negative NPV. This tells us that the project's rate of return is less than 6%. Therefore, let's rerun the analysis using a lower rate of return, such as 4% or 5%.

When we use 4% as the discount rate, we receive a present value of the benefits of $37,046. This is larger than the present value of the costs, therefore we know that the project is expected to earn more than 4%. We could stop here and interpolate, but let's try one more time to get as narrow a range as possible. When we use 5% as the discount rate, we receive a present value of the benefits of $35,893. Since this is less than the PVC, the project should earn less than 5%.

Since the project's rate of return is between 4% and 5%, let's interpolate to find the exact internal rate of return.

### *Interpolation*

4% 37,046 difference on top is X difference on top is 249 outside difference is 1% I.R.R. 36,797 outside difference is 1,153 5% 35,893. Interpolating to find the value of X, we set up a simple proportion:

X

1% = 249

1,153

X = 249

1,153

* 1%

X = 0.22%

The IRR is greater than 4% and 0.22% away from 4%. Therefore, the IRR must be equal to 4.22%.

g. Determine the modified internal rate of return (MIRR) for the new machine.

We determine the *future value* of the cash inflows and then solve for the rate of return that would equate the *present value of the costs* and the *future value of the inflows.*

CASH OUTFLOWS @ 6% CASH INFLOWS

(0) Cost of Asset 43,588 (1) 6,957 x 1.338 = $9,310

Transportation 800 (2) 8,570 x 1.262 = 10,819

Working Capital 1,412 (3) 7,072 x 1.191 = 8,423

Sale Proceeds (8,300) (4) 6,356 x 1.124 = 7,141

Tax on Sale of Old (703) (5) 6,059 x 1.060 = 6,422

(6) 7,247 x 1.000 = 7,274

*P.V. of Costs* = $36,797 *F.V. of Benefits* = $49,362

If the project costs $36,797 today and it generates cash of $49,362 after six years, what is the project's rate of return? We use the geometric mean return formula to solve for the rate of return:

5.02Rate of return 0.0502 or %

Rate of return 1.3415 -1

Rate of return 1.3415 -1

-1

$36,797

$49,362

Rate of return

-1

Beginning value

Ending value

Rate of return

0.166667

)6( 1

6

n

?

?

?

?

?

h. Determine the payback period for the new machine.

CALCULATION OF PAYBACK PERIOD

| Year | Cash Outflow | Cash Inflow | Amount Owed | No. of Years |
|---|---|---|---|---|
| 0 | $36,797 | | $36,797 | |
| 1 | | 6,957 | 29,840 | 1.00 |
| 2 | | 8,570 | 21,270 | 1.00 |
| 3 | | 7,072 | 14,199 | 1.00 |
| 4 | | 6,356 | 7,843 | 1.00 |
| 5 | | 6,059 | 1,784 | 1.00 |
| 6 | | 7,247 | 0 | 0.25 |

*Payback Period* = 5.25

The payback period is 5.25 years.

## MONTE CARLO METHODS IN FINANCE

In the fields of finance and mathematical finance, Monte Carlo methods are used to value and analyze basic financial models through to complex instruments, portfolios and investments by simulating the various sources of uncertainty affecting their value, and then determining their average value over the range of resultant outcomes.

The advantage of Monte Carlo methods over other techniques increases as the dimensions (sources of uncertainty) of the problem increase.

Monte Carlo methods were first introduced to finance in 1977 by Phelim Boyle in his seminal paper "Options: A Monte Carlo Approach" in the *Journal of Financial Economics.*

This article discusses typical financial problems in which Monte Carlo methods are used. It also touches on the use of so-called "quasi-random" methods such as the use of Sobol sequences.

## Overview

The Monte Carlo Method encompasses any technique of statistical sampling employed to approximate solutions to quantitative problems.

Essentially, the Monte Carlo method solves a problem by directly simulating the underlying physical process and then calculating the (average) result of the process. This very general approach is valid in areas such as physics, chemistry, computer science etc.

In finance, the Monte Carlo method is used to simulate the various sources of uncertainty that affect the value of the instrument, portfolio or investment in question, and to then calculate a representative value given these possible values of the underlying inputs. This approach is therefore used by financial analysts who wish to construct "stochastic" or probabilistic financial models as opposed to the traditional static and deterministic models.

Some examples:

- In Corporate Finance, project finance and real options analysis, Monte Carlo Methods are used to analyze the characteristics of a project's net present value (NPV). Here, the cash flow components that are (heavily) impacted by uncertainty are modeled, mathematically reflecting their "random characteristics". Then, as above, the average NPV of the potential investment - as well as its volatility and other sensitivities - is observed from the resultant histogram of project NPV; this histogram is effectively the project's probability distribution. (Typically, analysts use an add-in such as Crystal Ball to run Monte Carlo simulations in a spreadsheet environment.) See further under Corporate finance.
- In valuing an option on equity, the simulation generates several thousand possible (but random) price paths for the underlying share, with the associated exercise value (i.e. "payoff") of the option for each path. These payoffs are then averaged and discounted to today, and this result is the value of the option today; see Monte Carlo option model.

To value bonds - and bond options - the underlying source of uncertainty which is simulated is the (annualized) interest rate at which an entity can borrow money for a short period of time (i.e. the short rate). For each possible evolution of the interest rate we observe a different resultant bond price. These bond prices are then averaged, or are then the input for the valuation of the bond option. A similar approach is used in valuing swaps and swaptions.

- Monte Carlo Methods are used for portfolio evaluation. Here, the (correlated) behaviour of the component instruments is simulated over time, and the value of the portfolio is observed for each simulation. The various portfolio values are then combined in a histogram (i.e. the portfolio's probability distribution), and the statistical characteristics of the portfolio are then observed. A similar approach is used in calculating value at risk.

Although Monte Carlo methods provide flexibility, and can handle multiple sources of uncertainty, the use of these techniques is nevertheless not always appropriate. In general, simulation methods are preferred to other valuation techniques only when there are several state variables (i.e. several sources of uncertainty). These techniques are also of limited use in valuing American style derivatives.

## Applicability

### *Level of Complexity*

Many problems in mathematical finance entail the computation of a particular integral (for instance the problem of finding the arbitrage-free value of a particular derivative). In many cases these integrals can be valued analytically, and in still more cases they can be valued using numerical integration, or computed using a partial differential equation (PDE). However when the number of dimensions (or degrees of freedom) in the problem is large, PDE's and numerical integrals become intractable, and in these cases Monte Carlo methods often give better results.

For more than three or four state variables, formulae such as Black Scholes (i.e. analytic solutions) do not exist, while other standard approaches (i.e. numerical methods) such as the Binomial options pricing model and Finite difference methods face several difficulties and are not practical. In these cases, Monte Carlo methods converge to the solution more quickly than numerical methods, require less memory and are easier to program. For simpler situations, however, simulation is not the better solution because it is very time-consuming and computationally intensive.

## American Options

Monte-Carlo methods are harder to use with American options. This is because, in contrast to a partial differential equation, the Monte Carlo method really only estimates the option value assuming a given starting point and time.

However, for early exercise, we would also need to know the option value at the intermediate times between the simulation start time and the option expiry time.

In the Black-Scholes PDE approach these prices are easily obtained, because the simulation runs backwards from the expiry date. In Monte-Carlo this information is harder to obtain, but it can be done for example using the Least Squares algorithm of Longstaff and Schwartz.

## Monte Carlo Methods

### *Mathematically*

The fundamental theorem of arbitrage-free pricing states that the value of a derivative is equal to the discounted expected value of the derivative payoff where the expectation is taken under the risk-neutral measure.

An expectation is, in the language of pure mathematics, simply an integral with respect to the measure. Monte Carlo methods are ideally suited to evaluating difficult integrals (see also Monte Carlo method).

Thus if we suppose that our risk-neutral probability space is P and that we have a derivative H that depends on a set of underlying instruments $S_1,...,S_n$. Then given a sample $\omega$ from the probability space the value of the derivative is $H(S_1(\omega),S_2(\omega),...,S_n(\omega) = :H(\omega)$. Today's value of the derivative is found by taking the expectation over all possible samples and discounting at the risk-free rate. I.e. the derivative has value:

$$H_0 = df_T \int_\omega H(\omega)dP(\omega)$$

where $df_T$ is the discount factor corresponding to the risk-free rate to the final maturity date T years into the future.

Now suppose the integral is hard to compute. We can approximate the integral by generating sample paths and then taking an average. Suppose we generate N samples then

$$H_0 \approx df_T \frac{1}{N} \sum_{\omega \in SampleSet} H(\omega)$$

which is much easier to compute.

## Sample Paths for Standard Models

In finance underlying random variables (such as an underlying stock price) are usually assumed to follow a path that is a function of a Brownian motion. For example in the standard Black-Scholes model, the stock price evolves as

$$dS = \mu(t)Sdt + \sigma(t)SdW_t.$$

To sample a path following this distribution from time 0 to T, we chop the time interval into M units of length o*t*, and approximate the Brownian motion over the interval *dt* by a single normal variable of mean 0 and variance o*t*. This leads to a sample path of

$$S(k\delta t) = S(0)\exp\left(\sum_{i=0}^{i=k-1}\left[\left(\mu - \frac{\sigma^2}{2}\right)\delta t + \sigma \in_i \sqrt{\delta t}\right]\right)$$

for each k between 1 and M. Here each $\mu_i$ is a draw from a standard normal distribution. Let us suppose that a derivative H pays the average value of S between 0 and T then a sample path ω corresponds to a set $\{\mu_1,...,\mu_M\}$ and

$$H(\omega) = \frac{1}{M}\sum_{k=0}^{k<M} S(k\delta t)$$

We obtain the Monte-Carlo value of this derivative by generating N lots of M normal variables, creating N sample paths and so N values of H, and then taking the derivative. Commonly the derivative will depend on two or more (possibly correlated) underlyings. The method here can be extended to generate sample paths of several variables, where the normal variables building up the sample paths are appropriately correlated.

It follows from the Central Limit Theorem that quadrupling the number of sample paths approximately halves the error in the simulated price (i.e. the error has order sqrt(N) convergence).

In practice Monte Carlo methods are used for European-style derivatives involving at least three variables (more direct methods involving numerical integration can usually be used for those problems with only one or two underlyings. *See* Monte Carlo option model.

**Greeks**

Estimates for the "Greeks" of an option i.e. the (mathematical) derivatives of option value with respect to input parameters, can be obtained by numerical differentiation. This can be a time-consuming process (an entire Monte Carlo run must be performed for each "bump" or small change in input parameters). Further, taking numerical derivatives tends to emphasize the error (or noise) in the Monte Carlo value - making it necessary to simulate with a large number of sample paths. Practitioners regard these points as a key problem with using Monte Carlo methods.

## Variance Reduction

Square root convergence is slow, and so using the naive approach described above requires using a very large number of sample paths (1 million, say, for a typical problem) in order to obtain an accurate result. This state of affairs can be mitigated by variance reduction techniques. A simple technique is, for every sample path obtained, to take its antithetic path - that is given a path $\{\mu_1,...,\mu_M\}$ to also take { “ $\mu_1$,..., “ $\mu_M$}. Not only does this reduce the number of normal samples to be taken to generate N paths, but also reduces the variance of the sample paths, improving the accuracy.

Secondly it is also natural to use a control variate. Let us suppose that we wish to obtain the Monte Carlo value of a derivative H, but know the value analytically of a similar derivative I. Then H* = (Value of H according to Monte Carlo) + (Value of I analytically) - (Value of I according to same Monte Carlo paths) is a better estimate.

## Quasi-random (low-discrepancy) Methods

Instead of generating sample paths randomly, it is possible to systematically (and in fact completely deterministically, despite the "quasi-random" in the name) select points in a probability spaces so as to optimally "fill up" the space. The selection of points is a low-discrepancy sequence such as a Sobol sequence. Taking averages of derivative payoffs at points in a low-discrepancy sequence is often more efficient than taking averages of payoffs at random points.

# 3

# PRIVATISATION AND COMMERCIAL ACTS

## INTRODUCTION

This study examined the efficiency of privatization through the evaluation of financial performance of a privatized manufacturing company between the period 1978 to 2001. This period cover the pre-privatization and post-privatization period of the company under consideration. Privatization has been recognized as a key element to promote efficiency, reduce fiscal burden and help in developing capital market.

In order to achieve the objective of the study, secondary data on the performance indicators were collected from the annual reports of the organization. However, the findings showed that the privatization programme has a significant mixed impact on the operation of the company under study.

The programme also indicated a positive impact in the operating financial performance of the company as reflected in it's consistent growth rate of returns of the years under study, especially in post- privatization era of the company. In spite of the general positive impact of privatization on the financial performance of the company, the post-privatization period was beset with escalating operational cost resulting from high rate of inflation, which was seriously obstructing investment and industrial growth. Thus, policies to tame inflation should have inbuilt ability to increase the productive capacity of the company.

The privatization and commercialization Act 1988 (The Laws of the Federation CAP 369) introduced commercialization and privatization as measures for the re-organisation of state – owned enterprises in Nigeria. According to section 14 of the Act, privatization means "the relinquish- ment of part or all of the equity and other interests held by the Federal Government or its agency in enterprises whether wholly or partly owned by the Federal Government ..."

In order to deal with the general issues of reform, which apply to all Public Enterprises in Nigeria, government promulgated the commer- cialization and privatization Decree No. 25 of October, 1988. The Decree provides for the nece- ssary legal framework for planning, organization and implementation of government's anticipated programmes on public enterprises privatization as integral parts of Nigeria's on-going restructuring of its national economy. According to the Decree, the policy is aimed at the following objectives:

(i) restructuring and rationalization of the State- Owned Enterprises (SOEs) to lessen the dominance of unproductive investments in the sector;

(ii) re-orientation of SOEs towards a new horizon of performance, improvement, viability and overall efficiency;

(iii) ensuring positive returns on public sector investments in SOEs,

(iv) checking of the absolute dependence on the Treasury for funding SOEs and encouraging them to patronize the capital market; and

(v) initiation of the process of gradual cession to the private sector of such SOEs, which by their nature and type of operations, are best performed by the private sector.

At the inception of our nascent democracy in Nigeria, commercialization and privatization Act 28 of 1999 was enacted, which brought into existence the National Council on Privatization. However, the proposals for the reform of public enterprises (PEs) in Nigeria was based on the findings of the Onosode Commission (1984), government blamed the poor physical and financial performances of PEs in Nigeria on managerial inefficiency and incompetence. It is important to note that in most cases, particularly in the case of NEPA, product prices of PEs were subsidized to the tune of between 36% and 52% of the production cost in the pre- SAP period (Ayodele 1998:29). Thus, the continued deterioration of government's financial and fiscal posture especially in the mid 1980s when crude oil prices declined to below $10.00 per barrel, created additional financial difficulty for government to maintain its hitherto statutorily determined product prices which were below production costs. Thus, the continued precarious financial posture of government, coupled with the poor performances of PEs, offered a critical opportunity to challenge the wisdom in conti- nuously funding the PEs.

Against this background, the pervasive inefficiency and dismal financial failures of the PEs sector, therefore, raised vexing questions regarding the role and effectiveness of the state or government in the provision of those core services for which PEs were created.

Governments worldwide have been out- spoken on the need to foster private initiative in the interest of productivity and growth and have been taking substantive steps to move economic activities to the private sectors (Akinlo, 1998: 56-

65). In the developed world, some countries like France, Italy, Spain, U.K, Japan and USA have undertaken major privatizations. China, Brazil, South Korea, Bangladesh and Nigeria have all introduced privatization.

The decision to privatise some government enterprises was based on poor performance and inefficiency in the operations of public enterprises. Kikeri et al. (1994) noted that the high costs and poor performance of state-owned enterprises (SOEs) and the modest and fleeting results of reform efforts have turned many government towards privatization. The broad objective of this paper is to examine the pre and post-privatization financial performance of a manufacturing company, in view of the vital roles played in regulating the Nigerian economy in the manufacturing sector.

## PRIVATIZATION AND EFFICIENCY

Hall and Winstein (1959: 71-75) identify four categories of efficiency: efficiency in use; managerial efficiency, target or technical efficiency and return on equity capital. This has prevented a meeting of minds not only among management practitioners, but also among scholars. de Grazia (1961: 571), for example, calls attention to the value – orientation in the definition of the term "As an instrumental objective in administration, efficiency means that a given method of performing a task is most 'pleasing' to those controlling the method. Often 'pleasing' has to do with material values such as input-output ratio of machines, and clerks, but frequently the most efficient way of performing a task is conditioned on a clear triumph of executives' interests over the interests of others. Since scholars have been objected to the idea of using predetermined goals as a yardstick for measuring the relative success or failure of an organization. Etzoni (1960: 258) maintains that goal – attainment is not a fair test of an organization's strength.

Speight (1970: 1), in a more general way, says that an economic system was economically efficient so long as it was technically efficient and provided it succeeded in rationing out its scarce resources, and the scarce products of the resources, in the most desirable way. In any case, it is essential that an organization should fulfil certain objectives which are basic to its survival.

Balogun (1972. 21-34) argued that in Nigeria, the raison d'etre of many governmental or quasi-governmental organizations is being challenged simply because these organizations have failed to "deliver the goods" promised with the amount of resources at their disposal and within a given period. It is widely accepted that government enterprises are managed to achieve a variety of objectives that relate to the comp- lexities of politics, while private enterprises are largely managed to earn profits, and cost efficiency and market responsiveness are impor- tant to that pursuit.

The more competitive the markets in which the private enterprises operates, the more it is compelled by its objectives of profits and survival to operate efficiently (Willig, 1993: 155-180). According to Akinlo (1998: 56-65), the most widely vaunted argument for privatization is efficiency. His study revealed that evidence from the Nigerian experience shows that the fiscal and efficiency impacts of privatization have been low.

Performance evaluation in business according to Reid and Dubas (1978: 83-105) distinguish among various key aspect of performance measurement namely: economy, productivity, quality and level of service and effectiveness. From the existing literature, performance evaluation of a given firm could be done through intra or inter-company analysis. The inter- company analysis could not be easily achieved in Nigeria because of problem of inadequate data.

In Nigeria it is possible to adopt the intra-company analysis by adopting financial ratios which is simply the relationship between two accounting figures.

Woelfel (1979) suggests two ways of analysing the performance of a firm, namely, comparative financial statement and ratio analysis. According to Pandey (1981), ratio analysis helps the analyst to make qualitative judgement about the firm's financial position and performance in general. This study therefore seeks to appraise the performance of a privatized manufacturing company in Nigeria. Hence, the financial performance of the selected company operation, covered pre and post privatization era and therefore suitable for this study. The paper is divided into four parts. Part I provides the introduction to the study. In part II we discuss the methods of analysis adopted while in part III, we provide the analysis of data. Part IV contains the summary, recommendation and conclusion.

## METHODOLOGY

In view of the vital roles played in regulating the Nigerian economy, the food manufacturing industry is considered as a sample design of the study among 10 groups of privatized economic strata. To ensure accurate representation of the food sector, age was borne in mind while choosing the Flour Mills of Nigeria Plc as a case study.

The company was established in 1960 and started full operation in 1962. The grains grinding and the installed capacity of 3640 mlt per day make it the largest Flour Mills of Africa. It represents the first three generations of flour companies that have been privatized by the government.

Hence, the study concentrates on the financial performance of this company between 1978 and 2001 (pre and post privatization period). The data used in the study were obtained from the books of our chosen organization such as Annual Reports, the company's profile and indeed through personal interaction with the top executives in the organization.

The method of data analysis adopted was descriptive method. The analysis done in this study is to investigate the financial performance of a privatized manufacturing company using tables and financial ratios. The profitability ratios are the most appropriate tools to show the movement of each variable for the purpose of evaluating financial performance in the organization.

In evaluating the performance of the company, the following ratios were adopted:

(i) Asset turnover

This refers to the ratio of turnover to total Assets. It is a good indicator of management ability to generate income from available resources. It tells us the relative efficiency of the company.

ROA = Turnover x 100

Total Asset.

(ii) Return On Capital Employed (ROCE).

This is a fundamental measure of business performance. The ratio expresses the relationship between the net profit (before interest and taxation) generated by the business and the long-term capital invested in the business. It compares inputs (capital invested) with outputs (profit). This comparison is of vital importance in assessing the effectiveness with which funds have been deployed.

ROCE = Net Profit before interest and taxation x 100

Share capital + Reserves + Long-term loans

(iii) Return On Shareholders' Equity (ROE)

This ratio compares the amount of profit for the period available to the owners' stake in business. The ratio assesses profitability from the perspective of the corporate risk- taker. An upward trend indicates an increase in profitability, while a decrease indicates a decrease in profitability.

ROE = Profit After Tax x 100

Shareholders' Fund

(ordinary shares capital + reserves)

(iv) Gross Profit Margin (GPM)

This is calculated by dividing gross profit figure by the total sales figure. Gross profit represents the difference between sales and the cost of sales. This ratio indicates the efficiency of operation as well as how products are priced.

GMP = Gross Profit x 100

Sales

(v) Growth of Turnover

This shows the trend of turnover growth over the period under review.

(vi) Earning Per Share (EPS)

This ratio relates the earnings generated by the company during a period and available to shareholders to the number of shares in issue.

The trend in earnings per share over time is used to help assess the investment potential of a company's shares. For equity shareholders, the amount available will be represented by the net profit after tax (less any preference dividend, where applicable).

EPS = Profit After Tax

No. of Ordinary Shares in issue

## ANALYSIS OF DATA

Data presentation and analysis were based on the financial ratios computed and percentages derived from the financial statement/annual reports of the company under reivew.

The management of the company have been successful, year after year in taking advantage of the various available resources of income and these have been increasing at a slightly increasing rate over the years.

This general growth rate is higher in post-privatization era (between 1990 – 1994) relative to pre- privatization period.

The company's total assets have therefore, been well managed and made to perform considerably well at an increasing rate over the years under study. It has also experienced increased earnings and returns on total assets at increasing growth rate since the introduction of privatization programme of the Federal Govern- ment in the company.

In the pre-privatization period, the company experienced steady growth rate of return on capital employed, interspersed by a decline in growth rate in 1986 (17.2%) when ban was placed on the importation of wheat.

However, the company showed an upward trend i.e. the peak performance in terms of its efficiency in making return on capital employed in 1993 with 750.8% increase compared to 1992 with 54.7% increase upon introduction of privatization programme in the company.

The trend behaviour however, recorded a steady growth rate of return on capital employed from 1990 – 1998 (3.02% - 635.8%) with an interspersing decline from 1999 – 2001.

*Table: Pre-privatization performance criteria*

| Year | ROA % | ROCE % | ROE % | EPS K | GPM % | % Change in turnover |
|---|---|---|---|---|---|---|
| 1978 | 388.5 | 96.7 | 27.2 | 0.55 | 11.3 | |
| 1979 | 364.5 | 78.4 | 24 | 0.53 | 9.2 | -0.71 |
| 1980 | 384 | 88.2 | 18.6 | 0.44 | 9 | 14.87 |
| 1981 | 445.9 | 80.6 | 28.6 | 0.45 | 10.9 | 26.1 |
| 1982 | 503.9 | 68.4 | 18.6 | 0.32 | 7.5 | 22.5 |
| 1983 | 535.6 | 79.8 | 21.3 | 0 39 | 7 5 | 16 6 |
| 1984 | 478.9 | 60.4 | 14.8 | 0.29 | 6 | -5.2 |
| 1985 | 369.8 | 83.4 | 27 | 0.45 | 11.7 | -7.7 |
| 1986 | 221.1 | 17.2 | 6.2 | 0.11 | 3.9 | -38.4 |
| 1987 | 183.6 | 13.6 | 4.5 | 0.08 | 3.7 | -15.3 |
| 1988 | 182.6 | 20.7 | 7.8 | 0.14 | 3.3 | -3.1 |
| 1989 | 324.5 | 2 | 0.94 | 0.02 | 0.29 | 77.26 |

*Source:* Annual Reports and Accounts of the Company. (1978-1989)

In terms of Return on Shareholders Fund or Equity, ROE, the trend behaviour of the company showed an unstable or fluctuating rate of return in the pre-privatization periods over the years respectivelv but followed by decline in 1986-1989 (62 to 0.94%). The trend behaviour showed or indicated a peak performance in 1981 (28.6%). On the introduction of privatization progra- mme in 1989, the company recorded a slight growth in its ROE from 1.3%, 2.6%, 19.4%, 88.1% and 67.8% in 1990, 1991, 1992, 1993 and 1994, respectively. It was later followed by a decline from 47.3% and 20% recorded in 1995 and 1996 respectively. The trend behaviour still persisted till the year ended 2001 (18.5%).

In term of Gross Profit Margin (GMP) the trend behaviour in the pre-privatization era, the company experienced an unstable movement in growth rate with 11.7% in 1985 as at the peak performance in the period. Likewise, the post privatization period showed unstable movements in it's gross profit margin. The company however, attained it peak performance in 1998 with 12.8% in the post privatization period.

***Table: Post-privatization performance criteria under review. There were good levels in 1978-85***

| *Year* | *ROA %* | *ROCE %* | *ROE %* | *EPS K* | *GPM %* | *% Change in turnover* |
|---|---|---|---|---|---|---|
| 1990 | 477.8 | 3.02 | 1.3 | - | 6.1 | 28.9 |
| 1991 | 599.8 | 20.3 | 2.6 | - | 9.2 | 136.5 |
| 1992 | 1277.5 | 54.7 | 19.4 | 20.5 | 6.1 | 181 |
| 1993 | 1468.5 | 750.8 | 88.1 | 76 | 14.3 | 107.6 |
| 1994 | 1736.3 | 343.1 | 67.8 | 108 | 11.6 | -33.6 |
| 1995 | 811 | 321.9 | 47.3 | 107 | 19 | 138.2 |
| 1996 | 592 | 316 | 20 | 149 | 9.9 | 29.8 |
| 1997 | 708 | 311 | 17.7 | 107 | 9.6 | 29.8 |
| 1998 | 742 | 635.8 | 28.6 | 214 | 12.8 | 27.6 |
| 1999 | 874 | 307 | 16.9 | 92 | 11.8 | 6.9 |
| 2000 | 555 | 287.3 | 17.7 | 114 | 14.1 | 28.2 |
| 2001 | 650 | 354.7 | 18.5 | 132 | 11.8 | |

*Source:* Annual Reports and Accounts of the Company (1990-2001).

The trend of % change in Turnover showed an increase from 1979 – 1983 with 0.71%, 14.8%., 26.1%, 22.5% and 16.6% respectively. It however showed a negative trend behaviour from 1984 – 1988 with –5.2%, -7.7%, -38.4, -15.3% and –3.1% respectively. The trend behaviour later indicated the company's peak performance in 1989 with 77.3% increase. Upon privatization, the company recorded a slight growth in it's turnover from 28.9%, 136.5%, 181.8%,

107.6% from 1990 – 1993 respectively. The company's performance showed a negative performance in 1994 with –33.5% decrease. The company however started declining drastically from 1997 with 138.2% - 29.8% in 1998 and 1999.

The trend behaviour of EPS (Earnings Per Share) recorded a declining movement through- out the pre-privatization period. Upon-privatization, EPS of the company showed a great increase or upward movement compared to the pre-privatization period from 20.5K – 149K as the peak performance in 1996. The company in 1990 and 1991 did not make provision for earning per share from which dividend per share is computed. This implies that the company did not pay dividend to its shareholders' in 1990 and 1991 (i.e. all profit was retained by the company). Finally, in spite of the general positive impact of privatization on the financial performance of FMN, however, the company is still beset with prevailing escalating operational costs resulting from high rate of inflation which are seriously obstructing investment and industrial growth.

## SUMMARY AND CONCLUSION

This study examined the extent of the effectiveness of privatization on the company between the period of 1978 and 2001. This period cover the pre-privatization and post-privatization period of the company under consideration. The result showed that there have been upward trends and steady growth in post-privatization era based on ROA, ROCE and ROE but with slight fluctuation in the growth rate in some of the years under study. The same trend as stated above applied to EPS, GPM and Turnover for the years under study.

Some major problems that were encountered by the company prior to privatization especially the ban placed in the importation of wheat affected the performance of the company after privatization.

Moreover, the relative efficiency with which the organization utilized its resources in generat- ing revenue was weak during the period under review. By and large, the privatization programme had a significant mixed impact on the operation of the company under study. In both short run and long run, the privatization programme indicated a positive in the operating financial performance of the company as reflected in its consistent growth rate of return of the years under study in post-privatization era.

In conclusion, the potentials of privatization in enhancing efficiency need to be enhanced particularly in Nigeria. Evidence from the Nigerian experience shows that efficiency impacts of privatization have been low. It should be noted that the privatization policy has helped in stimulating and broadening the scope of the capital market. The following are recommended for survival and increased profitability of privatized government enterprises:

(i) restructuring and streamlining of companies' operations for purpose of efficiency, effectiveness and reduced cost structure.

(ii) determining of a competitive advantage and corporate planning to maintain those advantages vis-à-vis compe- titors in the economic system.

(iii) an improved internal control system that enables the fine- tuning of regulatory mechanism for enhanced integrity, efficiency and cost-effectiveness opera- tions with crippling initiative and innovations must be adopted.

4

# BUSINESS FINANCIAL PLANNING

Financial planning is the task of determining how a business will afford to achieve its strategic goals and objectives. Usually, a company creates a Financial Plan immediately after the vision and objectives have been set. The Financial Plan describes each of the activities, resources, equipment and materials that are needed to achieve these objectives, as well as the timeframes involved.

The Financial Planning activity involves the following tasks;-

- Assess the business environment
- Confirm the business vision and objectives
- Identify the types of resources needed to achieve these objectives
- Quantify the amount of resource (labor, equipment, materials)
- Calculate the total cost of each type of resource
- Summarize the costs to create a budget
- Identify any risks and issues with the budget set

Performing Financial Planning is critical to the success of any organization. It provides the Business Plan with rigor, by confirming that the objectives set are achievable from a financial point of view. It also helps the CEO to set financial targets for the organization, and reward staff for meeting objectives within the budget set.

## INTRODUCTION

A key element of planning is financial planning. Most businesses will need to borrow to set-up and this will mean developing a financial plan. This will probably be required by most lenders before they will decide whether to lend to you. In this section we look at how you can go about preparing a financial plan - from calculating break-even output, through to the preparation of cash flow forecasts and projected balance sheets and profit and loss accounts. Follow the links below to look in more detail at each of the steps necessary to prepare a financial plan.

- Step 1 - Break-even - how many of your product will you need to sell before you break-even?
- Step 2 - Cash flow forecasting - a vital element of a financial plan is the development of a cash flow forecast. This can help identify how much money you may need to borrow and more importantly - when you may need it.
- Step 3 - Financial statements - you will also need to produce a projected balance sheet and profit and loss account to show the expected financial performance of your business. How do you go about producing these and what are they?

There is a business planning case study that you may like to have a go at when you have looked through each of these sections.

### Step 1 - Break-even

There is a lot of confusion about break-even analysis. The following information will hopefully allay some of those confusions! Importantly you should NOT confuse break-even with supply and demand analysis! Break-even is a useful planning tool for a business. Break-even is the output level where total costs equal total revenue.

A vital part of any business plan is to see what output level or sales level is necessary before you are going to break-even. Break-even does not specify a time that it will take to reach this level. This will depend on how quickly sales are generated. In some cases it can be many years before a firm would reach its break-even sales level. A bank or other investor will almost certainly want to see break-even information. To work out break-even we need to know various bits of information:

1. The price you are charging
2. The variable costs (direct costs) of each unit - these are the costs of raw materials, labour and so on that can be directly attributed to each unit.
3. The fixed costs (or indirect costs/overheads) - these are the costs that stay the same whatever the level of output and will be things like rent, marketing costs, admin costs and so on.

Once we have this information, we can work out the break-even level of output. Let's look at an example:

Price = £5

Variable costs = £3 per unit

Fixed costs = £1,000

From this information we can see that every time we sell one more unit we have an excess of income over variable costs of £2. We call this figure the contribution. However, this is NOT the same as profit, because we still have to pay the fixed costs of £1,000. We therefore need to work out how many we need to sell for the total contribution to be equal to the fixed costs. In this case, the contribution is £2 per unit and the fixed costs are £1,000, so if we can sell 500 units then we will have had enough contribution to pay the fixed costs. Any units we sell beyond that level will then make a profit of £2 each. So if we sell 501 units, our total profit will be £2. If we sell 502 units our total profit will be £4 and so on. The break-even level of output can therefore be calculated from the following formula:

Break-even output =Fixed costs Contribution (per unit)

However, we can also work out the break-even level of information by plotting the figures on a graph. To do this, we need to go through the following steps:

### *Stage 1*

Plot the total cost line - remember this will be the sum of the fixed costs and variable costs. This means that it will start from part way up the y-axis because of the fixed costs.

### *Stage 2*

Add the total revenue curve. This can be plotted by working out the total revenue at the maximum capacity of the firm, e.g. if they can produce 50,000 units of a good and they sell them at £28 each, then the TR line will go from the origin to a point given by 50,000 units and £1.4m.

The diagram should now look like this:

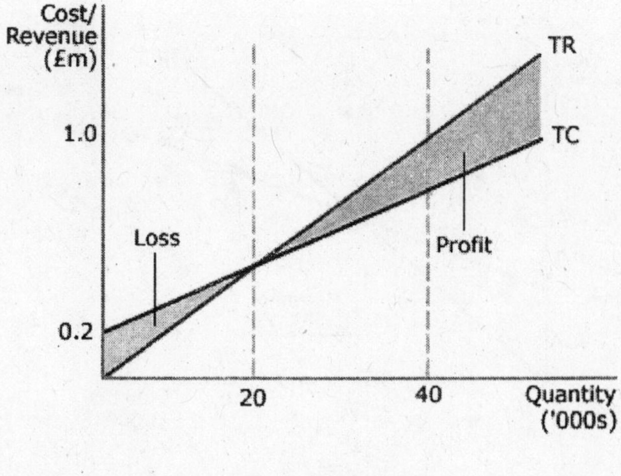

### *Stage 3*

The point where the TR and TC lines cross is the break-even level of output. At this point the firm will break-even. Any level of output above this point they will make a profit, but any level of output below this point they will make a loss. We can see this from the diagram below:

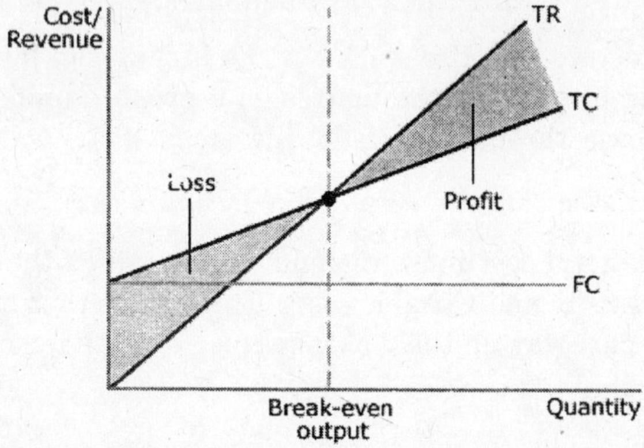


### *Stage 4*

We can also identify from the diagram the margin of safety of the firm. The margin of safety shows how far from break-even output the firm is currently producing. It shows, in other words, how much output could fall before the firm started making a loss. We can see the margin of safety on the diagram below:

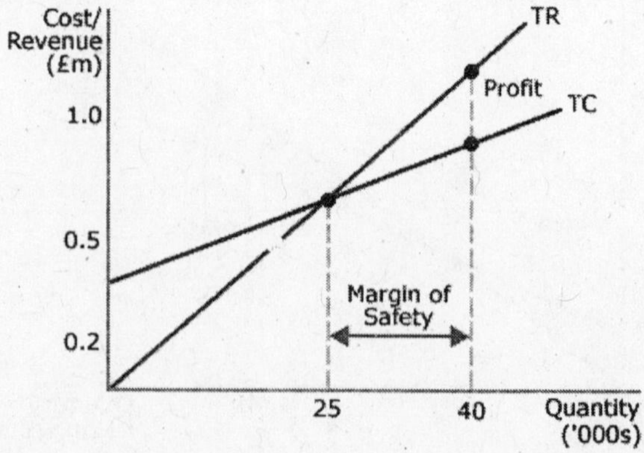

On the diagram below, estimate the company's position if it produced 10,000 units. The total revenue from selling 10,000 units would be £0.2m. The total cost of producing 10,000 units would however be £0.42m. The company would therefore be making a loss of £0.22m if it continued producing at this level.

However, if it increased output and sales to 20,000 units, then the revenue would rise to £0.4m and the costs of producing 20,000 units would have risen (because of the variable costs) to £0.5m. The fixed costs of producing 10,000 units and 20,000 units are however the same so the revenue is rising at a faster rate than the costs. The loss at this level of sales therefore would be £0.1m. This figure is lower than the loss made at 10,000 units. If you follow through the logic here you can identify the level of profit or loss at different levels of sales and output.

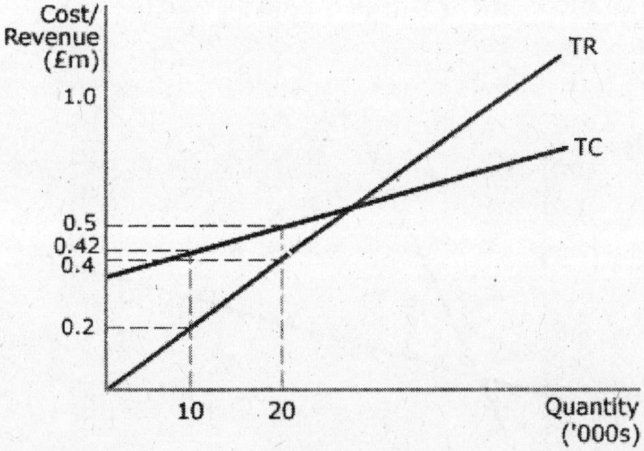


This is all based on an assumption about the structure of the total revenue curve. Total revenue is price times the quantity sold (TR = P x Q). If the business decided to charge a different price, the total revenue curve would be a different shape. If the company decided to charge a lower price, the total revenue curve would be flatter. This would mean that the company needs to sell a greater volume before they will break-even. It does not mean that they will never sell enough, it merely means they have to sell more.

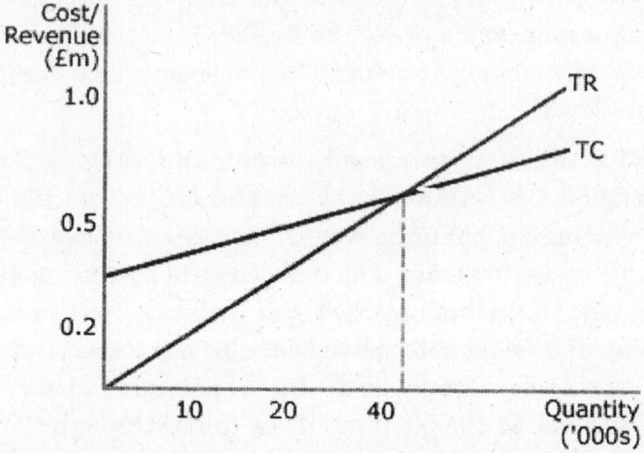


On the other hand, if they decided on setting price at a higher level, the TR curve would now be steeper. This would imply that the number of sales needed to break-even would be less.

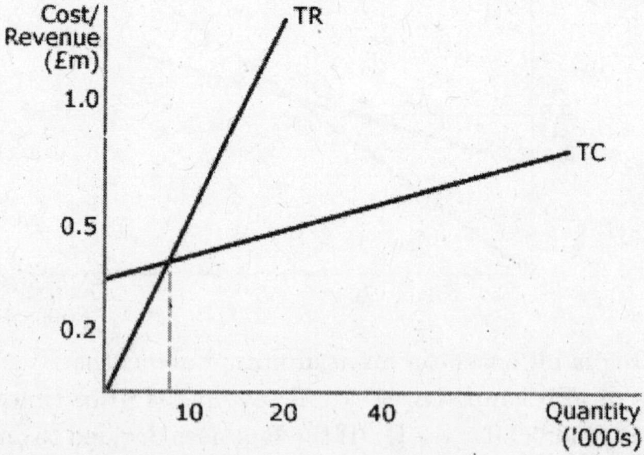


The decision on the price level will depend on a host of factors - the level of competition, the type of product and what market it is aimed at (for example, is the product aimed at groups A and B in the 'social class groupings' or at a mass market?) and the results of market research conducted by the company that may inform their decisions. Using break-even analysis therefore allows a business to be able to plan and be informed of the impact of its decisions.

Break-even analysis is therefore an example of a quantitative decision making technique. The decision on the actual price to charge will largely be a qualitative one albeit based on other forms of information such as the results of market research

## Step 2 - Cash flow forecasting

There are two types of cash flow statement that you will come across, these are:

- Actual cash flow statements - these show an historic view, showing the actual flows of cash into and out of a business that have occurred over a previous trading period, e.g. 6 months, or 1 year.
- Forecast cash flow statements - these show the expected flows of cash into and out of a business over a trading period in the immediate future, e.g. next 6 months or year.

When looking at preparing a business plan, it is obviously the second of these that we will be doing, and generally businesses are more concerned about forecasting cash flow, as this helps them to see the need for any short-term financing.

### *Preparing a Cash Flow Forecast*

The cash flow forecast essentially has three separate parts to it. They are:

1. Projected revenue

2. Projected expenses
3. Balance

When planning your business, you will need to draw up figures for each of these items, so think carefully about how many you think you will sell and when and what all your possible expenses will be and when they will need to be paid.

Remember the cash flow shows when the cash is actually paid or received - this is not necessarily at the same time as the sale or purchase is made.

Let's look at an example. Let's say you have forecast the following, and the business will be starting on January 1st next year:

- Sales will be £950 per month, but with one month credit given, so the cash is received one month after the sale is made.
- Expenses will be:
  - o Rent - £200 per month - payable immediately
  - o Raw materials - £100 per month - but with one month credit given
  - o Wages - £250 per month - payable each month
  - o Rates - £400 per quarter - payable every three months (first payment in January)
  - o Electricity - £55 per quarter - first payment in March
  - o Travelling - £75 per month - payable immediately
- The opening business bank balance will be £250

From this information we can prepare a cash flow statement for the first 6 months of the business. Have a look at the table below and check you could reproduce this.

| | January | February | March | April | May | June |
|---|---|---|---|---|---|---|
| Revenue | | | | | | |
| Sales | — | 950 | 950 | 950 | 950 | 950 |
| Expenses | | | | | | |
| Rent | 200 | 200 | 200 | 200 | 200 | 200 |
| Raw materials | 100 | 100 | 100 | 100 | 100 | 100 |
| Wages | 250 | 250 | 250 | 250 | 250 | 250 |
| Rates | 400 | 0 | 0 | 400 | 0 | 0 |
| Electricity | 0 | 0 | 55 | 0 | 0 | 55 |
| Travelling | 75 | 75 | 75 | 75 | 75 | 75 |
| Total expenses | 925 | 625 | 680 | 1025 | 625 | 680 |
| Net cash flow | -925 | 325 | 270 | -75 | 325 | 270 |
| Opening balance | 250 | -675 | -350 | -80 | -155 | 170 |
| Net cash flow | -925 | 325 | 270 | -75 | 325 | 270 |
| Closing balance | -675 | -350 | -80 | -155 | 170 | 440 |

We can see from this forecast that in the first few months of operation, the business is going to need some sort of short-term finance, but by May, they have a positive bank balance.

Perhaps the most appropriate way to finance this would be through an overdraft arrangement, as they believe it will be short-term.

## Step 3 - Projected financial statements

A bank or any other potential investor looking at your business plan will almost certainly expect to see projected financial statements (along with a cash flow forecast).

The two main financial statements that you would normally include are a balance sheet and a profit and loss account. In this step we look at the construction of a balance sheet and a profit and loss account.

### *Profit and Loss Account*

A profit and loss account is a statement of the trading performance of a firm over a period of time. It is usually shown for a year (as by law all limited companies have to produce these), though companies may produce internal ones to assess their progress more frequently.

A profit and loss account is normally laid out as follows:

Profit and loss account for Biz Training Ltd. For the year ended 30th April 2005.

| | **30.4.2004** | **31.4.2005** |
|---|---|---|
| Turnover (1) | 3,200 | 4,000 |
| Cost of sales (2) | 1,400 | 1,600 |
| Gross profit | 1,800 | 2,400 |
| Expenses (3) | 1,400 | 1,600 |
| Depreciation (4) | 40 | 100 |
| Net profit | 360 | 700 |
| Interest | 100 | 100 |
| Profit on ordinary activities before tax | 260 | 600 |
| Taxation | 40 | 160 |
| Profit after tax | 220 | 440 |
| Dividends (5) | 100 | 140 |
| Retained profit (6) (to balance sheet) | 120 | 300 |

The previous year is often given beside the current year to enable comparison.

### *Notes*

1. The turnover is the total sales figure for the period, i.e. the total revenue received or sales revenue - you might see all these terms used interchangeably!
2. The cost of sales is the direct or variable costs. These are raw materials, labour costs (that can be directly

attributed to output) and any other direct production costs for the product.

3. Expenses are the other costs that are not directly attributable to output. These are usually termed the indirect (fixed) costs or overheads.
4. Depreciation is a charge to the profit and loss account to allow for the fall in value that has taken place in fixed assets as they are used up. Depreciation can be charged in a number of ways including the reducing balance or straight-line methods.
5. Dividend is the share of profit that is paid to the shareholders as the reward for their capital. They are after all the owners of the business and so receive their share of the profit as a dividend.
6. Most companies retain some of the profit for use to help expand and grow the business - this figure is the profit after tax less the dividend and is called the retained profit. It is added to the balance sheet as part of the profit and loss account entry there.

### *Balance Sheet*

In contrast to the profit and loss account the balance sheet is a snapshot of the financial situation of the firm at a given moment in time. A balance sheet, as its name suggests, contains two parts which should balance, i.e. be the same value. One half shows what the company actually owns at that point in time (its assets) and the other shows where the money has come from to pay for those assets. In the assets section we have to recognise that at any point in time the company will also have money that it owes to other people (liabilities) - this has to be subtracted from its assets. These two halves of the balance sheet should balance as they simply show where the money has come from and where that same money is being used - hence the name balance sheet! A balance sheet is generally laid out as follows:

Balance sheet for Biz Training Ltd. as at 30th April 2005.

| | 30.4.2005 (£ 000) | |
|---|---|---|
| Fixed assets (1) | | |
| Land | 150 | |
| Buildings | 280 | |
| Plant and equipment | 360 | 790 |
| Current assets (2) | | |
| Stock (3) | 200 | |
| Debtors (4) | 45 | |
| Cash | 35 | 280 |
| Current liabilities (5) | | |
| Creditors (6) | 250 | |
| Overdrafts | 140 | 390 |
| Long-term liabilities (7) | | |
| Long-term loans (over 1 year) | 350 | 350 |
| Net assets | | 330 |
| Source of funds | | |
| Share capital (8) | 200 | |
| Retained profits (9) | 130 | |
| Capital employed | | 330 |

As you can see the net assets in the top half of £330,000 match the capital employed in the bottom half of £330,000.

## *Notes*

1. The fixed assets are the assets that will last for more than a year. This might include buildings and machinery. It is these assets on which depreciation is charged in the profit and loss account.

2. The current assets are made up of stocks, (goods not yet sold) debtors (those who have yet to pay the business for supplies/goods, etc. they have purchased) and cash and are assets that can be realised (sold) relatively quickly - certainly in less than a year.
3. Stock includes stocks or raw materials, any work-in-progress and also any stocks of finished goods that are waiting to be sold.
4. Debtors are people or firms that owe money to the company. The company wants to ensure that it collects these debts as promptly as possible to ensure a good cash flow through the business.
5. Current liabilities are short-term liabilities. That is, they are money that is owed by the firm to someone else. A large part of this is often creditors (suppliers who are owed money), but it may also include overdrafts or short-term loans.
6. Creditors are firms or people who the business owes money to.
7. Long-term liabilities include money that is owed to someone else or another firm, but is not due to be repaid for more than a year. This may include longer-term loans from banks or other financial institutions.
8. Share capital is the capital that was raised when the shares in the business were originally sold.
9. Retained profits are the total level of profit that has been kept in the business over the years and not paid out to the shareholders. Each year this will increase by the amount of the retained profit in the profit and loss account.

## STRATEGIC PLANNING

When undertaking a new business venture or expanding into new territory, it is important to have strategic planning sessions in order to foresee possible issues, outcomes, and ways of dealing with each phase that will need to be completed.

Because these projects are usually large in scope, there may be many phases to be completed. This means during strategic planning sessions, a time line will have to be determined. Regardless of whether a company plans on completing a larger project by itself or hiring strategic consultants, planning in advance will save money and help reduce confusion surrounding a new project.

As technology continues to improve, there are many tracking programs, engineering programs, and business writing programs that can aid project leaders and group members in completing their tasks. Companies should consider investing in this software in order to compete with other companies, and as a way for employees to become more productive.

Before beginning any project, it is important to select project managers, group members, and decide which planning software to use. Using software is one business strategy that will help track the progress of group members, track budgets, and help coordinate time lines with other groups that may be involved.

Once these concerns have addressed, deciding which group members will handle different tasks is the next step. Project managers usually know which each of their group's strengths and weaknesses and are able to match them with tasks that fall within their knowledge base. If a group is working with a new project manager, they may have to tell them their areas of expertise in order for these decisions to be made.

Financial planning for any project should never be ignored, but this is particularly important for large projects. The strategic management team will have to discuss various ways to keep spending within the budget and where to find additional funds if the budget falls short. The financial planning stage is very important because if there isn't enough to finish the project, then it may be delayed until a later time. While this may not the goal of too many, it is a good business strategy if the project will take too much money to complete.

The financial planning stage should include funds for materials, labor, time, and profits the company expects to make after the project is complete. While financial planning cannot predict the outcome of the final cost for all projects, it can give project mangers an estimate of how much they will be able to spend.

Included in the business plans for the project should be financial planning, project phases, time lines, group members involved, and any other information that can be used during the project.

There are many ways to write a business plan, but many companies use business plan software and plug in the information they have available. Not only does this save time, but it also ensures that the plan is as clear as it can be.

Unclear business plans can lead to overspending and other issues later on. Strategic planning consultants can be used during this phase of the project as well by offering advice on how to write a business plan and reviewing it to make sure all issues are addressed.

A strategic plan may be reviewed once the project is completed to make sure that all areas have been covered. They will also be studied to see how closely strategic planning measures were followed.

Projects that went over budget, were understaffed, or planned too quickly will fall under scrutiny. Business strategies may be called into question and better planning sessions will be required in the future. This is why project managers and strategic consulting agencies emphasize the importance of proper planning.

While there are many levels to strategic planning, the most important one seems to be financial planning. Because finances dictate the amount of people who will be able to work on a project and the time in which it can be completed, a financial planner may be needed to help organize and prioritize each phase of a project.

By carefully reviewing the amount spent on different phases, financial planning experts will be able to make recommendations on how to save money, where to spend more money, and when to spend. Depending on the size of the project and the amount a company expects to make once the project is complete will determine how much they are willing to spend.

Business planning can be stressful for all involved, but it is a necessary practice in order for companies to remain successful. This is why companies invest in strategic consulting experts who are able to give opinions that are unbiased and helpful.

There are many stages of business planning as there are in maintain projects. This is because of the amount of research that must be done in order to see a project through to completion. Researching what is best for a company is a strategy that a business should use first before proceeding with any project.

After researching the benefits and the risks involved with a project, then strategic planning committees can be formed who will review all research and make recommendations. A business that uses strategic planning techniques and strategy management as a way to decide if a project is worth pursuing is a company that invests wisely in its future and in its employees as well. Carelessly spending money on projects that do not benefit a company will only lead to future disasters along the way.

Financial planning and strategic planning are effective tools used by many companies. Hiring consultants to help prepare materials, lead discussions, and offer advice have helped many companies become more profitable. Keeping clear documentation concerning all phases of a project can help companies learn from their mistakes and their successes. Document managers are used to preserve and store these documents for future use. Once a project has been completed, it will be reviewed by using these documents. This is a common business strategy that makes a company stronger than it was before.

5

# BUSINESS PLANNING AND FINANCIAL FORECASTING

## INTRODUCTION

You want to start a business – or expand your existing business. You have a great idea, super attitude and the entrepreneurial spirit. So you head down to your local bank; you sit down in front of the credit manager and start to explain this brilliant idea when she interrupts you, *"That sounds great, but where is your* business plan?"

This scenario is played out every day in Canada. People with ideas – in many cases good ideas – who want to plunge into the business without having even done the business plan. The purpose of this publication is to explain in simple terms the concept of the business plan and to show you how to put your own plan together. There is all sorts of help available to you – including the other books in the Solution Series, courses from your local college or school board and of course the Interactive Business Planner.

### Why do a Business Plan?

You should do a business plan for a number of important reasons. Some of those reasons include:

- Your own thinking process is solidified through the planning process. The planning outline leads you through a series of questions and issues that you may have forgotten about when just thinking about your business. *Remember that you are* an investor in your own business. You are the first person who must be convinced of the validity of your business concept.

- Your bank will need to be convinced of the viability of your business, or your business expansion. The business plan is a *communications tool*. Inform and influence the reader towards some action – providing a loan, extending credit or investing in your business.
- Your business plan provides some guideposts in running your business. You will set goals and then, once you are in business, you can measure those goals against the actual performance. Goals should be specific, measurable, achievable, realistic and time limited – SMART.

Your business plan has three elements. It *prepares* you – the entrepreneur for starting the business.

It *explains* your business and *proves* the viability of the business to outside parties. It spells out your business *goals* in clear SMART terms.

## What is in a Business Plan?

There are as many kinds of business plans as there are kinds of businesses. There are dozens of planning guides and planning outlines, books, audio tapes, computer programs and online planning services. All of them have things in common and all have differences. (In researching this publication, the author never ran across two business planning outlines that were identical.) The business outline presented here is very simple. It has a reader friendly flow. It is not written in stone. If there are areas you need to add, then add them. If there are areas that need to be deleted, then delete them. If you are writing for a bank, then find out which sections are important to the bank. Most banks have excellent information on getting a business loan.

The reader reads what the writer writes You cannot assume that the reader of your plan knows anything beyond what you have stated in the plan. You may know what you mean. The question is have you clearly explained it to the reader? As you go through this outline, constantly ask yourself if you are making yourself clear to a reader who is not familiar with your industry or your business.

Your business plan is often your only representation to an outside party such as the bank!

Here are a few tips on the actual writing of the plan:

To Do

- Try to keep it under twenty pages, exclusive of the appendix.
- Use bullet points and numbered lists wherever possible.
- Use, but do not overuse, graphs, diagrams and photographs.
- Have a neutral third party read the plan – especially someone without a background in your industry.
- Please – for the reader's sake include a table of contents and page numbers in your plan.

***Avoid***

- Big words and long sentences. They only serve to confuse the reader.
- Technical words and unnecessary jargon. If you need to introduce a technical term, then you should define the term.
- Using acronyms and initials to express words is another common error.

You may be very familiar with the acronym but your reader might not. If an acronym has become as common as a word, such as scuba or laser, then use them. If they are still technical, such as URL then you may need to define the acronym and its meaning. Now that you have some background on the concept of the plan, we can look at the elements of the business plan.

The purpose of the executive summary is to get the readers attention by summarising the key elements of the business plan. It must be short, to the point and very well written. This is arguably the most important part of the business plan. The Introduction must encourage your reader to keep reading.

It is a good idea to write as much of the Introduction as you can at the outset of the planning process. This initial writing will help you to focus your attentions on the goals of the plan. You should then rewrite the Introduction after you have completed the rest of the business plan. This way the specifics of the plan, and the changes made during the planning process are accounted for.

### *Business Concept*

- Describe what your business does in general terms.
- Describe what differentiates your business from others.
- Briefly describe your business history if applicable.
- Provide any other information that will excite the reader about your business.

### *Plan Objective – Key Goals*

- Tell the reader what you want (i.e. a business loan for a specific amount to purchase equipment.)
- State your sales, production and profit goals.

- If this is for a bank loan, comment on goals such as anticipated time to positive cash flow and the ability to service debt. (Note you cannot complete this section until the rest of the plan is complete.)

### *Management / Ownership*

- Describe the technical qualifications of each principal in this enterprise.
- Describe the business qualifications of each principal in this enterprise.
- Tell the reader your business structure (i.e. proprietorship, partnership, and incorporation.)
- Provide a fact sheet with contact information such as name, address, telephone, e-mail etc.

### *Product / Service*

**Purpose:** The purpose of the product / service section is to detail exactly what your business does for the customer and what makes these offerings desirable to the customer.

### *Key Products (Goods Businesses)*

- Describe each product you sell. This is your product mix.
- If you cannot list each product, break the business down into logical categories.
- Describe the key product features, and how your products are different from those of your competition. (Functionality, durability, ease of use etc.)
- Describe product protection such as patents, copyrights and trademarks.

### *Key Services (Service Businesses)*

- Describe each type of service you offer. (Be specific)

- Describe the service features in terms important to the customer.
- Describe any service protection such as copyrights or trademarks.

### *Product Risks*

- If there are any risks associated with your product or service such as product liability, professional liability, or ease of duplication by competition, state them and show how you will avoid these risks.

### *Industry & Market Research*

**Purpose:** The purpose of the Industry & Market Research section is to prove that the market is large enough, in your area, given the competition to support the survival and growth of your business.

### *Industry Research*

- Describe your industry. The less well known the industry, the more description necessary.
- Describe the state of the industry. Is it a new industry, growth industry, competitive industry, or a stable mature industry?
- Document industry trends on a world or national size. Sales, number of customers, number of units sold, trends in related industries are all good industry indicators.
- Describe the key customers *for your specific industry.*
- Provide other national / international economic indicators that encourage the health of your industry.
- Examine risks to the entire industry caused by legislation, technological change or any threat to the industry as a whole.

## Target Market – Customer Research

The *Target Market* is the groupings of consumers or businesses most likely to purchase your products or services. The first group you plan to target is your *Primary Target Market*; the second is your *Secondary Target Market*. It is very important that you understand your target market – after all these are the customers you need to keep happy!

### *Who is the customer?*

(Provide both the description and the information in this section.)

- Age
- Gender
- Income
- Family Status

Be sure to include how many customers there are in each grouping

- Industry Type
- Size of Customer
- Annual Sales

Estimate the number of companies using directories or Yellow Pages.

Where is the customer? Target the geographic radius of your customer base by city, region province or country. The geography of business to business markets tends to be larger than consumer markets.

When do they buy? Is there a particularly busy season for your product or service i.e. Christmas?

If you are selling to seasonal businesses, the timing can be everything i.e. wholesaling.

What do they buy?

- Necessity
- Luxury Item
- High involvement / Big ticket
- Low involvement / consumable
- Capital Item
- Inventory Item (i.e. item that is resold)
- Consumable Item

Why do they buy? How does your product or service help the consumer?

How does your product enhance the performance of this business?

How much do they buy? Determine how much is spent on your product by your customers.

Estimate the commercial expenditure by the industries in your target area.

**Consumer Markets Business Markets**

Note: If you are using indirect distribution, it may be necessary to describe both your customer as a target market, and the end user as a target market.

- Provide the results of any customer survey work you have done
- Provide the sources of information for any of the above

***Competitive Analysis***

- List the direct competitors in your local market. These are firms who offer exactly what you offer. List the current number and the number in existence for the past three-year period.

- List the indirect competitors in your local market. These are firms who offer substitute products.
- Analyse any competitors who have gone out of business in the past and if possible why.
- Explain how your firm will compete with these competitors to prove how you can survive in their markets.
- Examine risks that could occur when you enter the market. For example what if your key competitor cuts their price when you open your business?
- Show how your products / services or how your company is different from your competition. (This is called positioning your product.)

### *Marketing (Market Strategies)*

**Purpose:** The purpose of the Marketing section is to demonstrate how you plan to tap your market. This includes pricing, distribution, sales and promotional strategies.

### *Price Strategy*

- What are your prices for different products and services?
- How did you arrive at those prices? (Charge going rate, industry standard mark-up etc.)
- Do you have any "price packages"?
- What is your price image? (Bargain, middle of the road, high end) Is this consistent with your target market?
- How do your prices compare with your competition?
- Have you accounted for mark-downs and off price promotions?

## Physical Distribution

Describe which of the following distribution systems you plan to use in your business:

- Direct Distribution – selling directly from producer/ provider to the customer.
- Wholesale Distribution – selling to a retailer who sells to the customer.
- Brokers or Agents – using a third party to sell the product – usually on a commission basis. This can be done for goods (Manufacturers Agents) or for services (Speaker's Bureau).
- Hybrid Distribution – Using more than one of the above.
- Internet Sales – See Internet Strategies Section.

Location (For retail, restaurant and location dependant businesses)

- Neighbourhood Location (use map). Traffic counts and supporting information such as population radius is helpful.
- Site Location – place in mall or centre, or city block. Show the other tenants and access / egress for parking if applicable.
- Facility Location – including a diagram of the business layout.
- Signage both inside and outside the business.
- Check for location risks. A median placed in the middle of your road will cut off access to your business. Check with your city-planning department before signing a lease.

## Promotion

Your promotional strategy is made up of three main areas. Not all businesses use all three so only include the parts relevant to your situation.

### *Advertising Plan (Paid Advertising)*

- Provide a list of the media you plan to use. You may include newspapers, magazines, radio, television, direct mail or Internet advertising.
- Develop a monthly advertising schedule with planned budgeted amounts.
- If you have written any ads or brochures, include them as appendices to the business plan.

### *Public Relations Plan*

- Include media sources you plan to use to promote your business.
- Include press releases in the appendices to the business plan.
- If you are using a Public Relations firm indicate the name of the firm in this section.

### *Personal Selling Plan*

- Describe how you will prospect and find new customers.
- Describe how you will fulfil these prospects with information.
- If you have letters of agreement, contracts or other sales tools, it is sometimes advisable to include them as appendices to the business plan.

### *Internet*

The Internet is becoming increasingly important to today's business world. Industry Canada uses a consumer benefit model known as ICET. You should define your Internet strategy in the same way with the following:

- Information Gathering – This includes the information provided to the consumer about your business, products and services.

- Communication – This includes more specific forms of two-way communications such as customer service and feed back mechanisms.
- Entertainment – This is the multimedia aspect approach to your site. This includes animation, sound clips and video clips.
- Transactions – This is the ability to actually order and pay for products over the Internet.

### *Operations*

**Purpose:** The purpose of the Operations section is to indicate how you plan to operate the business. That means how you provide the services or provide the products.

### *Production Plan*

The production plan demonstrates your ability to produce products. This section may not apply in service businesses.

### *Production Flow Chart*

(Manufacturing businesses)

- Provide a flow chart / process diagram showing the entire production process from start to finish.
- List and budget production equipment required for the business.

Procurement (Businesses that manufacture or sell products)

- Sources of supply and order lead time
- Terms & Conditions of sale
- Alternate sources of supply (this addresses procurement risk)
- Inventory control systems
- Physical space requirements (Unless covered in location sections)

Sub Contractors (These can include both goods and services)

- Provide a list of sub-contractors
- Show exactly what these subcontractors do and where they fit into the production of the business
- Show alternative sub contractors (This addresses sub-contract risk)

Human Resources (If you have more than five staff members)

- Organizational Chart (Show reporting structure)
- Job Descriptions (Show what people do)
- Job Specifications (Show the skills and knowledge required to do each job.)
- Recruiting – Where will you find good people?
- Management – How will you treat those good people?
- Compensation – How much will you pay your people? This includes base wages, commissions, bonuses and other incentives. (Don't forget your statutory benefits of EI, CPP, WCB & Holiday pay, in addition to any benefits you plan to add.)
- Human Resources Risks. Look at contingent plans for loss of key personnel, labour shortages or strikes.

Professionals and Mentors – where the entrepreneur turns for help

- Accountant
- Lawyer
- Banking Services
- Business Advisors and Mentors (It can be helpful to provide brief one paragraph biographies on key business advisors.)

### *Legal & Administrative*

- Legal Form (proprietorship, partnership, corporation, cooperative.)
- Share Distribution (Corporation Only)
- Directors & Officers (Corporation Only)
- Buy Sell Agreement (Corporation and Partnerships Only)
- List of key legal agreements such as contracts, leases, agreements, franchise agreements, personal loan guarantees etc. (The actual documentation is often put into the appendix of the business plan.)
- Insurance / Risk management

The financial plan is critical to the success of your business plan – especially if it is for the purpose of getting a bank loan. The Cash Flow Forecast is arguably the most important part of the plan – however, each of the other documents is important from a planning perspective.

### *The Break-even*

The break-even point in your business is the point at which your sales revenue is equal to your total expenses. At that point you neither make money, nor do you loose any. The breakeven lets you know what it is going to take in sales just to survive. It provides a good indication of the viability of a business project. The break-even can also be used to evaluate a business expansion or any other business expenditure. You are simply asking how much additional revenue will be required to cover the additional cost.

There are some key definitions necessary to determine the break-even for the business. They are:

Fixed Costs (Overhead) are costs that do not vary directly with sales. Utilities, salaries, advertising, office supplies and telephone are just a few examples. They do not have to be the same every month. What is important is that you pay them regardless of sales made.

Variable Costs (Cost of Goods) are the actual costs of making the product or providing the service. They can include materials, shipping and contract labour. Capacity governs your output. It can be measured in units of production, billable hours, or sales volume.

To calculate the break-even in units – we use the following formula:

This method is known as *Total Absorption Costing*, because dividing the total cost by the units sold absorbs the fixed costs. This allows us to compute the *break-even* for this business. Every business plan – be it for growth or for start-up – needs to establish project and business costs before proceeding.

Note: For planning purposes treat the entire term loan payment, both principal and interest, as a fixed cost to the business. Fixed Costs

(Unit Price – Variable Cost) = Break-even in units

### *Illustrative Example*

Jan is a home-based potter who makes custom mugs by the case. Her *capacity* is no more than 15 cases of mugs per week. She has calculated the *variable* cost for each case, including clay, glaze and packaging to be $50 per case. It costs Jan $3,000 per week to run her business, including her wage. The cost per case, when we include the $3,000 per week *in fixed costs*, changes depending on the number of cases produced each week. This is calculated in the table below.

Notice that the break-even is not a point, but it varies for each different price point. If she can get $425 per case for her mugs, she needs to be able to produce and sell eight mugs per week. We can plot this on a graph as follows: The area above the line is profit and the area below the line represents loss.

### *Break Even with a Gross Profit Margin*

Sometimes, a company does not sell products, if it sells so many different products that doing a break-even for each unit does not make sense. When this is the case, such as in a retail business, we calculate the break-even in revenue rather than in units. This is done with the following formula:

Where:

There are industry standard financial ratios available from Statistics Canada for many small businesses. These ratios include the gross profit margin, expressed as a percent of sales.

| Units Produced | Fixed Costs | Variable Costs | Price Per Unit |
|---|---|---|---|
| 5 | $3,000 | $250 | $650 |
| 6 | $3,000 | $300 | $550 |
| 7 | $3,000 | $350 | $479 |
| 8 | $3,000 | $400 | $425 |
| 9 | $3,000 | $450 | $383 |
| 10 | $3,000 | $500 | $350 |
| 11 | $3,000 | $550 | $323 |
| 12 | $3,000 | $600 | $300 |
| 13 | $3,000 | $650 | $281 |
| 14 | $3,000 | $700 | $264 |
| 15 | $3,000 | $750 | $250 |

Fixed Costs

Gross Margin = Break-even Sales

(Price – Cost)

Price = Gross Margin

***Illustrative Example***

Sarah wants to start a retail gift store. She estimates her *monthly fixed costs* at $9,000 per month. She determines that the industry standard *Gross Margin* for a gift store is 45%. She calculates her break-even as follows: Sarah must be convinced that this location is able to sell at least $20,000 per month (or $240,000 per year) before she starts her business. Her market research, physical location, promotional plans and physical size must all support this level of sales capacity or the business will not work.

The break-even is a great first step in evaluating business opportunities. It is not that the objective is to break-even, but that the break-even is the first objective to achieve in reaching a profitable business.

## The Balance Sheet

The *Balance Sheet* is a snap shot of the business at any point in time. In the case of a business start-up, it is often the *starting balance sheet.* A balance sheet is made up of three parts.

*Assets:* Things a business owns

*Liabilities:* Debts a business owes

*Equity:* The owners' investment and re-investment in the business

Everything that the business owns, its assets have to have been paid for. Therefore we get the following formula.

*Assets = Liabilities + Equity*

This is extremely important as it gives the reader a picture of how the business is being financed through the owners' money (equity) or through the creditors money (liabilities). In a business start-up you should look at the assets required to get the business started – and then ask yourself how you will finance that start-up. If you do not have the money to invest into the business, you will have to borrow the remainder.

*Fixed Costs*

Gross Margin = Break-even Sales $9,000

45% = $20,000 per month

X Proprietorship

*Balance Sheet*

December 31, 2000

*Assets Liabilities*

Current Assets Current Liabilities

Cash $ 2,000 Trade Payables $ 2,000

Inventory 15,000 Wages Payable 3,000

Accounts Receivable 12,000 Line of Credit 4,000

Total Current Assets $ 29,000 Total Current Liabilities $ 9,000

Capital Assets Long Term Debt

Vehicle $ 20,000 Term Loan $ 10,000

Less Accumulated Depreciation (5,000) Note Payable 6,000

Book Value (Vehicle) 15,000 *Total Long Term Debt* $ 16,000

Equipment 15,000 Total Liabilities $ 25,000

Less Accumulated Depreciation (3,000) Equity

Book Value (Equipment) 12,000 Owners Equity $ 31,000

*Total Capital Assets* $ 27,000 Total Liabilities & Owners Equity $ 56,000

Total Assets $ 56,000

*The Income Statement Forecast*

The purpose of the *Income Statement Forecast* is to project the revenues and expenses of your business over a given period of time – usually one year. Other terms for this are *budgeted income statement* or *pro forma income statement*. There are three things that need to be predicted to forecast your income statement: the sales projection, the cost of goods projection and the overhead's projection.

### The Sales Forecast

The sales forecast is probably the most difficult part of the business to forecast – especially for a starting business. Sometimes, the break-even can provide a starting point for creating the sales forecast. It is important to remember that a sales forecast is not like the weather – something that you try to guess – but rather a goal you set for the business that you proactively try to achieve.

In the case of an existing business, you should look at the sales history. You should see if your sales are trending up or down, and then account for new products to be added, or old products to be taken away. *The sales* forecast must reflect your business strategies and objectives.

### Forecasting using the Unit Method

List all the products or services you plan to sell. You will need to forecast the number of units of each type you plan to sell. Different businesses and industries use different unit measures. (E.g., for a craftsperson, a unit may be one wooden item; for a researcher, a unit could be one hour of time.) You will have to estimate the selling price for each unit. You can then develop a sales forecast using the following equation: A business owner will do a sales forecast for each product in the business. The sum of these forecasts becomes the overall sales forecast.

### *Forecasting with the Sales Method*

Sometimes a business cannot use unit sales, as it would be impossible to predict the unit sales for each of 5,000 items in a gift store. In this case, some business owners will go directly to revenue forecast. If the business is broken down into logical departments or categories, then forecast the revenue in each area for the total sales forecast.

### *The Cost of Goods Forecast*

The cost of goods forecast relates directly to the sales forecast. The cost of producing goods varies directly with the level of sales. To calculate the cost of goods forecast, you may use either the percent to sales method, or the unit costing method.

### *Unit Costing Method*

This method is exactly like the unit sales forecast, except instead of using price, you use cost per unit.

Just as in the unit forecast, you must do this for each unit sold. The sum of the cost of goods is then part of the income statement.

*Total Sales = Number of units sold* x *Price per unit*

*Cost of Goods = Number of units sold* x *Cost per unit*

### *The percentage cost method*

In retail businesses – where mark-ups and mark-downs predominate it is common to use the *cost complement* to calculate the cost of goods. The cost complement is the percent of the revenue, or the selling price, which represents the cost of goods. For example, if an item costs $12.00 and is priced at $20.00 then the cost complement is $12.00 / $20.00 = 60%. (If the *cost complement* is 60% then the *Gross Profit Margin* is 40%.) You can use the historical cost complement or industry standards to forecast the cost of goods and gross profit of your income statement.

### *The Overheads Forecast*

The overheads forecast is an estimate of your *expenses* for the year. This list should be similar to the list developed for the fixed costs of your break-even analysis. Typical overhead expenses include:

- Advertising and Promotion
- Automobile
- Bank & Finance Charges
- Communications
- Depreciation
- Insurance
- Entertainment & Meals
- Occupancy
- Mail & Office Supplies
- Professional Fees
- Professional Development
- Wages & Benefits
- Travel & Accommodations
- Other
- Owners' Drawing or Wage

The next step is to make cost estimates for each area. You may do them monthly, or annually, however, you will eventually need to know your monthly expenditure in each area for your cash flow forecast. Some of your forecasts will be a matter of calling a supplier and asking for a quote – insurance is an example of this kind of overhead. Sometimes, you will have to make a management decision about how much you will plan to spend in order to achieve your revenue objectives. If you have history, you should use history as a guide, making sure that increases and decreases in cost are consistent with your revenue objectives.

You should make a brief note to the reader of the plan, describing the key expense forecasted items. (i.e. you may have a quote from a broker for your insurance projection.) This is especially true if, in an existing business, there is a large change in the statement.

Sample Income Statement

X Proprietorship

Income Statement

Year Ending December 31, 2001

Sales $84,100

Less Cost of Goods $15,000

Gross Profit $69,100

Expenses

Advertising $ 1,500

Depreciation $ 8,000

Interest $ 2,000

Rent $ 4,000

Travel $ 600

Wages $ 7,000

Total Expenses $23,100

Net Profit $46,000

(Gross Profit – Total Expenses)

Less Owner's Draw $15,000

Net Profit after Draw $31,000

Note: The term draw in a Proprietorship refers to the money that the owner takes out of the company. The profits kept in the business are known as *retained earnings*. These earnings are reflected in the owners' equity portion of the balance sheet. It should also be noted that in a proprietorship, income tax is paid on the *net profit – not the owner's draw*.

### *The Cash Flow Forecast*

A *Cash Flow Forecast* is probably your most important financial tool. It is your cash flow that shows you if, and when, you will run out of cash essential to run your business. It allows you to take action before problems occur and even to do "what if " calculations before taking on new projects. The cash flow is a 12-month projection that forecasts the *receipts* and *disbursements* for your business. In a start-up situation, it is preferable to have a start-up month to specifically show the reader the costs incurred to start the business.

### *Why Do a Cash Flow Forecast?*

Too often business owners do a cash flow forecast in their head. Putting the cash flow forecast on paper, however, will give you the following:

- A format for planning the most effective use of your cash (cash management).
- A schedule of anticipated cash receipts – follow through to see that you achieve it!
- A schedule of priorities for the payment of accounts– stick to it!

- A measure of the significance of unexpected changes in circumstances; e.g., reduction of sales, strikes, tight money situations, etc.
- A list, on paper, of all the bill paying details which have been running around in your head, keeping you awake nights. A cash flow is not an instant cure for sleeplessness but it certainly helps. It also clears your mind for more productive thinking.
- An estimate of the amount of money you need to borrow in order to finance your daytoday operations. This is perhaps the most important aspect of a completed cash flow forecast. • An outline to show you and the lender that you have enough cash to make your loan payments on time.

### *Receipts*

Receipts occur when cash enters the business for any reason. It is like making a deposit in your current account. The main reasons for receipts are:

- Cash sales
- Collection of accounts receivable
- Loan proceeds. This includes term loans, start-up loans, line of credit and notes.
- Owners' contributions. This includes both investments and shareholders' loans (Shareholders' loans only happen in incorporated companies.)

### *Disbursements*

Disbursements occur when cash leaves the business for any reason. The main reasons for disbursements are:

- Cash expenses or inventory purchases
- Payments of accounts or expenses payable
- Loan repayment (Either bank or shareholders' loans)

- Owner repayment (Dividends in a corporation or drawings in a proprietorship)

In cash flow, we talk about receipts, disbursements and deficits or surpluses rather than revenue, expenses and profits or losses.

### *How to do your Cash Flow*

The cash flow is made up of three distinctive parts. The receipts, the disbursements and the cash flow calculation. Because of the complexity of the disbursements section, this section has been broken down into a series of smaller sections. Each line is coded with a letter and a number. The letters form the following sections on your cash flow sheet:

A – Receipts

B – Disbursements for Inventory Purchases and Sub-Contracted / Piecework Labour

C– Disbursements for Overhead Expenses

D – Disbursements for Capital Purchases

E – Repayments of Bank Loans, Notes, and Investors

F – Cash Flow Calculation

In addition, there are two schedules – the monthly sales / accounts receivable forecast, and the inventory purchases forecast. These forecasts will be inserted into lines A1& A2 and B1&B2 respectively.

### *Start-up – For business start-ups only*

The *Start-up* column is used in start-up situations only. It is used for all of the receipts and disbursements that occur as a part of starting a business. This includes purchasing fixed assets, incurring start-up expenses, the initial investment to start the business and the initial bank loans. It is helpful for the reader to separate start-up costs from on going costs. This way they will quickly see why you may have large deficits in the early stages of business development.

Using *Start-up* makes your cash flow easier for a reader to read. (You should be able to spot the starting balance sheet right off of *Start-up* in a business start –up.)

### *A – Receipts*

The sales and accounts receivable section is forwarded directly from Schedule 1. Any owners' investments and loan proceeds are put into the appropriate row. Note that some lines of credit are forwarded in $5,000 increments. Others are treated as overdrafts. Both methods can be used in section A. One example of other receipts is sales of a fixed asset.

### *B – Disbursements for Inventory*

Purchases and Sub-Contracted / Piecework Labour

This section is forwarded directly from Schedule 2.

Sometimes you can replace all of the materials you use up in a given month. When this is the case, your purchases are equal to your cost of materials for each month. Other companies need to build up inventory. This can be caused when your productive capacity is lower than your highest sales month. You build up inventory so you can meet orders in peak periods. You will need to do an inventory forecast, based on your sales and your production.

*Beginning of Month Inventory (B1.1)* This is taken from either the balance sheet or from the previous month's end of period forecast.

*End of Month Inventory (B1.2)* This is the target inventory level for the end of the month. It is based on the seasonal needs of the business and allows you to compensate for rising and falling inventory levels.

*Cost of Material (B1.2)* This is the cost of the material taken from inventory and sold to customers. (Note it is accounted for at material cost only).

*Purchases (B1.4)* This is the amount of material required to replace material used and bring the inventory level to the end of month target.

To calculate the purchases, use the following formula:

End of Month Inventory (B1.2) + Material Used (B1.3)- Beginning of Period Inventory (B1.1) = Purchases (B1.4)

The End of month Inventory figure is then forwarded to the line Beginning of Month Inventory for the next month. This procedure is repeated for the entire 12-month cycle. If you have credit terms from your suppliers, you should then make an adjustment for your accounts payable (B1).

This usually involves purchasing in one month and paying for it the next.

Piecework labour (B2) is forecast in conjunction with your monthly production.

### *C– Disbursements for Overhead Expenses*

The C section is the cash outflow of your overhead expenses. If you pay your entire insurance in one month, then the entire amount is disbursed in that month. Some disbursements are the same every month, such as rent. Some disbursements will be similar to your sales pattern– advertising might be an example. Some disbursements are quarterly such as income tax instalments or, in some businesses, the GST.

*Note: it is a good idea to* disburse GST & PST into a separate holding account until they need to be remitted to government. This way the money is there when you owe it rather than having been used up in normal business operations.

### *D – Disbursements for Capital Purchases*

If you plan to purchase any capital assets at any time, account for these purchases in the D section. If you do not pay for the asset right away, remember to put the amount into the month in which you plan to write the cheque.

### *E – Repayments of Bank Loans, Notes, and Investors*

The cash flow does not discriminate between principal and interest. The entire payment on term loans will be brought forward to the cash flow.

If there is interest on lines of credit or on overdrafts they should be accounted for here. In the same way as some lines of credit are forwarded in $5,000 increments – they are repaid in $5,000 increments. You should also account for any repayment of shareholders' loans, owners' draws not accounted for in wages, or dividends in the appropriate row of section E.

### *F – The Cash Flow Calculation*

The cash flow calculation (detailed on your cash flow sheet) is Starting Cash Balance + Total Receipts – Total Disbursements = Ending Cash Balance Now you can adjust your cash flow and your business strategies, to ensure that you do not run out of cash – or exceed pre-arranged lines of credit and overdrafts.

### *Financing Your Business*

There are two main types of financing – equity financing and debt financing. *Equity* means ownership. With equity financing, an investor makes money available for use in exchange for an ownership share in the business. This could be as a silent or limited partner (not actively involved in the business) or as a shareholder. Whether equity financing is possible or a good option depends on the business structure and relationship between the borrower and lender.

With debt financing, the lender charges interest for the use or 'rental' of money loaned, but does not get a share or equity in the business. Debt financing is familiar to most people because it is the basis of most personal credit. Debt often comes from banks, but it can also come in the form of supplier credit (accounts payable) or in the form of vendor credit – for capital purchases.

### *Bank Financing*

Many entrepreneurs will go to the bank for part of their business financing. This can be financing the start-up of the business or financing the growth of an existing business. Either way, bank financing plays a major part in the development of small business. Banks use many different kinds of financial instruments to finance business. The two main types are Lines of Credit and Term Loans. *Line of Credit* is a loan similar to a personal overdraft. It is to finance temporary shortages in cash caused by inventory and accounts receivable.

They are sometimes disbursed into your chequing account in increments of $5,000. The interest rates are often variable and based on the prime lending rate. As a rule *lines of credit finance current assets. Term Loans* are loans that are repaid over a fixed period of time – usually more than one year. A business may have several term loans at the same time – financing different projects or assets. Term loans may or may not have fixed interest rates, depending on the terms and conditions. Usually, term loans are used to finance capital assets, although sometimes term loans are taken out to increase cash levels (current assets) in the business.

### *Lending Criterion*

Many banks use the four "C's" to evaluate loan proposals. They represent:

**Cash Flow:** The ability to repay the loan with cash. This is measured using the Cash Flow Forecast in your business plan.

**Collateral:** The value of internal and external security that may be liquidated. This is measured by taking the market value of the business assets and comparing this value to all outstanding term debts. This determines what might happen if the business defaults on the loan. Sometimes an asset outside of the business will secure a business loan. This is external security. An associated company may hold the asset or it may be a personal asset of the business owner. (See loan guarantees.) Character: Aspects about the business owner or owners, which lead you to believe in their credit worthiness. Banks often use the business owners' personal history to determine attitudes towards credit. They will also look at the technical and business skills presented in the business plan.

**Commitment:** The financial commitment by the owners in this business venture. This is measured by examining the equity or shareholders loans in the business, and the retained earnings history of the business.

## *Statement of Personal Net Worth*

A statement of personal net worth is a measure of the wealth of the owner or owners of the business. It is similar to a balance sheet – except those assets are measured at their market value. The formula for net worth is: Net Worth = Assets (Market Value) – Liabilities

## *Personal Loan Guarantees*

When a small corporation borrows money from a bank, the shareholders will often be required to sign what is known as a personal loan guarantee. This is like the individual co-signing a loan granted to the corporation. It means that if the corporation (business) defaults on the loan (that is banker's language for not repaying the loan) then the individual shareholders must re-pay for the corporation. It is not unusual for the spouses of shareholders to sign guarantees as well. This prevents the guarantor (the person who signs the guarantee) from transferring their net worth to their spouse. Personal loan guarantees are required for most business loans. Always remember that the guarantee is a legal document, and it is advisable to see a lawyer before signing any such document.

### *Program & Financing*

The program and financing is a description of the loan requirement and the asset purchase. It looks like a small balance sheet in that it states what you are going to purchase, and how you are going to pay for it.

Supposing that X Proprietorship wants to purchase a $5,000 piece of equipment. They decide to borrow $3,000 use $1,000 of the businesses cash, and invest an additional $1000 into the company. The starting balance sheet, program & financing and pro-forma balance sheet would look like this:

The program and financing and the statements of personal net worth must be provided along with the business plan to ensure the creditworthy nature of the business venture.

Initial Balance Sheet

Program & Pro-Forma

Financing Balance Sheet

Assets

Current Assets

Cash $ 2,000 -$1,000 $ 1,000

Inventory $ 15,000 $ 15,000

Accounts Receivable $ 12,000 $ 12,000

Total Current Assets $ 29,000 $ 28,000

Capital Assets

Book Value (Vehicle) $ 15,000 $ 15,000

Book Value Equipment $ 12,000 $ 5,000 $ 17,000

Total Capital Assets $ 27,000 $ 32,000

Total Assets $ 56,000 $ 60,000

Liabilities

Current Liabilities

Trade Payables $ 2,000 $ 2,000

Wages Payable $ 3,000 $ 3,000

Line of Credit $ 4,000 $ 4,000

Total Current Liabilities $ 9,000 $ 9,000

Long Term Debt

Term Loan $ 10,000 $ 3,000 $ 13,000

Note Payable $ 6,000 $ 6,000

Total Long Term Debt $ 16,000 $ 19,000

Total Liabilities $ 25,000 $ 28,000

Equity

Owner's Equity $ 31,000 $ 1,000 $ 32,000

Total Liabilities & Owner's Equity $ 56,000 $ 60,000

### *Appendices*

Purpose: The purpose of the appendices is to provide supporting documents for claims made in the business plan. They may not necessarily be read, but are there for research purposes.

- Resume(s) of Principals

- Legal documents (including leases, insurance etc.)
- Letters of agreement / intent (potential orders, customer commitments, letters of support)
- Sample Ads and brochures
- Collation of Market Surveys
- Other

Your banker or a potential investor may request the following documents:

- Personal net worth statement (including personal property values, investments, cash, bank loans, charge accounts, mortgages, other liabilities; this will substantiate the value of your personal guarantee if required for security)
- List of inventory (type, age, value)
- List of leasehold improvements (description, when made)
- List of fixed assets (description, age, current market value of any equipment; legal description of any lands; description of any encumbrances on assets to be pledged for business purposes)
- Price lists (to support cost estimates)
- Description of insurance coverage (insurance policies, amount of coverage)
- Accounts receivable summary (include ageing schedule)
- Accounts payable summary (include schedule of payments)
- Copies of legal agreements (contracts, lease, franchise agreement, mortgage, debentures)
- Appraisals (include recent appraisals of assets such as buildings, property, and equipment or provide a

market evaluation of the business and an asset list outlining the asset, the year purchased and amount paid)

- Financial statements for associated companies (where appropriate)
- Name of present lending institution (branch, type of accounts)
- Lawyer's name (include address and phone/fax number)
- Accountant's name (include address and phone/fax number)

The following information will be a specific part of a loan application:

- Name lenders, amount of financing and payment periods for short-term and long-term loans
- Term loan applied for (amount, term, when required)
- Owner's equity (your level of commitment to the program)
- Line of credit applied for (new or increased, security offered)
- Present financing including term loans outstanding and current operating line of credit
- Total all amounts from

'Owners/Investors/Shareholders' and 'Lenders' for total sources of financing.

List uses of financing with amounts and totals. These could include:

- Land
- Buildings and facilities
- Equipment and machinery

- Remodeling, renovations and Leasehold Improvements
- Initial inventory
- Working capital (for operating expenses)
- Non-liquid assets contributed by owners

**Note:** The total amount in uses of financing should be the same as the total for sources of financing. Most of this information should also have been determined in the financial plan, but will often need to be re-stated for the loan application.

### *Some Final Thoughts*

Dwight Eisenhower once said: *"In preparing* for battle, I have found that plans are useless, but *planning is indispensable."* Starting a business is a great undertaking. You want to be prepared. So here are some tips to keep in mind while in the planning process:

- Keep an open mind. Do not try to make something work that cannot work, just because you like the idea.
- Be flexible – whilst developing the business plan other ideas, markets, products or services may come to mind. Explore them.
- Make your mistakes on paper – it is far cheaper than making them in real life.
- Keep planning! It can be difficult to plan when you are running your business, but it is very useful to re-examine your goals and objectives on a regular basis. Don't ever let the business squeegee out the creative entrepreneur.

## INVESTMENT AND FINANCIAL PLANNING IN INDIA

Investment and financial planning in India has been successful to a very large extent, as is evident from the fact that in the present scenario, India is the 5th largest economy of the world. The market in India offers very high potential for earning and growth in all the spheres of business. All this has been possible due to the proper financial and investment planning in India. The Ministry of finance regulates all the investment and financial planning in India. It is this ministry that formulates all the rules and regulations that are to be followed for financial investment in the country. The National Common Minimum Program was formulated by the government of India, for planning investments and finances in India. This program had identified certain sectors which must be given more emphasis in order to boost investments and economic growth of the country. The National development council is an agency which had been set up by the Indian government in order to boost financial and investment planning in India.

The Indian Planning Commission, in the 4th and 5th five-year plans, has implemented investment and financial planning in India in such a manner that it has given huge amounts of resources to the states. But in the 9th and 10th five year plans, this financial assistance given to the states has been cut down sharply.

In the planning of finance and investment in India, the 9th five year plan did not lay down a definite investment pattern. Due to this it was not possible to gauge the investment requirements in the various sectors, the amount of investment that was likely to take place, and the sectors that will have insufficient or excess of funds.

In the 10th five year plan in India, investments had to be cut by 12.5% in important areas like manufacturing, agriculture, and power due to constraints in resources. However, it cannot be denied that Investment and financial planning in India has helped the country to grow economically.

# 6

# GAINING COMPETITIVE ADVANTAGE THROUGH ENTERPRISE PLANNING

No matter how good its products or innovative its services, no organization can perform to its full potential without an adequate planning structure in place. Allowing enterprises to allocate their most precious (and finite) resources—money and people—in response to changing conditions and objectives, today's enterprise planning solutions facilitate a dynamic planning process that both promotes best business practices and spawns new ones. These solutions provide the enterprise planning tools that organizations need to maximize their resources and execute their business strategies.

## INTRODUCTION

In today's fast-paced business environment, planning has to entail more than a once-a-year activity. If managers are to perform the thoughtful analysis and what-if projections essential to smart decision-making, planning needs to be an ongoing dynamic activity that promotes collaboration across departments and organizational layers, and links budget allocations to real-world drivers. However, to derive the wide spectrum of business benefits availed by this type of best practices enterprise planning—such as more tightly aligned operations and strategies, shorter planning cycles, and more-predictable financial performance— companies must implement new technologies. Out-of-date planning tools simply cannot link planning processes and data across the enterprise, facilitate collaboration among all process participants, or provide critical capabilities (such as drilldown and what-if scenario management) in the way that today's sophisticated enterprise planning technology allows. By taking advantage of advances in enterprise planning technology, organizations can transform an annual exercise that adds little value to the business into one that ensures the continuous optimization of resource allocations and the consistent, effective execution of the business strategy across the enterprise.

## A BRIEF HISTORY OF PLANNING

Before the advent of computers, companies performed planning tasks with paper spreadsheets and calculators—a "technology" that required documents to be physically sent between locations and that provided no means of automatically linking values among documents. Planning, in other words, entailed a completely manual process—slow, error-prone, and extremely inflexible.

The advent of PCs and desktop spreadsheets, however, brought about a revolution in the way organizations planned and managed their budgets. For the first time, users could produce planning documents that could be easily shared and updated. In addition, those documents could contain far more information, graphics, and detail than previously possible.

### Special Purpose Budgeting Applications

With users enthusiastically adopting spreadsheet software, technology vendors soon began enhancing them with specialized budgeting applications that could handle compound growth rates, currency variables, and other factors beyond the purview of traditional spreadsheets. Suddenly, organizations were able to quickly and reliably build planning documents based on more-sophisticated (and thus more-accurate) models. And for the first time, they were able to plan across multiple dimensions of a business—among product lines, for example, and across various pay grades within a department.

These calculation-related enhancements, however, did not address fundamental planning issues such as process management, auditing, and the linkage between planning documents and key enterprise data sources—such as applications for enterprise resource planning and human resources. They also relied on distributing and collecting budgeting "files" between finance and business planners.

**Web-Enabled Applications**

The advent of the internet brought another wave of technological change to enterprise planning. Now, instead of having a fat client application distributed across the enterprise, an organization could provide browser-based access to shared planning databases and documents. And the documents could be maintained on a central Web server rather than dispersed across multiple users' desktops. This Web-enabled architecture provided significant process advantages over its desktop predecessors.

With documents maintained in a central location, version control and auditing could be introduced into the planning process. And because these documents were now stationary, budget values could be automatically populated with data from other documents and systems, and triggers could be set to automatically notify managers about thresholds and variances. However, management and integration capabilities were limited, and planning remained largely a static, top-down exercise rather than a dynamic process linked to core business applications and processes.

### What's Still Missing?

As evident from this overview of planning's history, advances in corporate planning practices are largely contingent on advances in planning technology: Each stage of technological advance has yielded important enhancements in how business users collaborate to optimize the allocation of corporate resources.

Despite these advancements, however, corporate planning has yet to reach its zenith. Many issues remain, and it is only by embracing the next generation of enterprise planning technology that businesses will be able to further enhance their planning processes and reap substantial performance benefits as a result.

## A LOOK INTO PLANNING'S FUTURE

What does next-generation enterprise planning technology look like? What differentiates it from previous generations of planning tools? And how does it enable organizations to implement proven planning best practices? Although each organization applies best practices in its own way to suit its unique business requirements and culture, any company operating in today's highly competitive, compliance-conscious business environment should demand the following functionality form their next-generation planning technology:

- Dynamic real-time updates. Business moves too quickly for management to rely on annual or quarterly numbers alone; allocation decisions and forecast revisions must instead be based on events and conditions that can change at any time. Next-generation planning environments make it easy to adjust to frequently (or even continuously) changing conditions by providing automated Web-based links to planning drivers across an enterprise. As a result, events or initiatives in one part of the organization can quickly and accurately drive appropriate responses in other parts of the organization. This dynamic approach eliminates the lag times and disconnects associated with conventional planning tools and traditional annual and quarterly planning.

- Multitiered aggregation and granularity. From the boardroom to the project team, planning takes place on many levels, which means that aggregation can become a nightmare if every team at each level uses a separate planning system. Even worse, it can be virtually impossible for upper management to drill down from an aggregated document to discover underlying issues. And finally, manually aggregating multiple spreadsheets introduces the possibility of gross human error. This is why the next generation of planning solutions unifies planning in a single environment, linking data across all organizational levels, departments, and functions.

Integration with enterprise applications and datasources. Everything from sales pipelines to labor rates, material costs, interest rates, currency exchange rates, and more can affect an organization's planning and budgeting. With data of this nature typically available from enterprise resource planning systems, human resources applications, external information services, and other sources, businesses need to be able to tap into these sources dynamically to adjust planning variables to reflect changing conditions—and they want to use familiar tools, such as Microsoft Office, to do so. A good next-generation enterprise planning solution will provide the integration interfaces and variable adjustment functions that are required to fulfill these needs.

- Translation between financial and nonfinancial metrics. Best practices accounting depends on organizationwide user collaboration. Web-based clients foster this by distributing application functionality wherever it's needed. It's equally important, however, to involve managers and team members who think in terms of operations rather than currency-quantified budget spreadsheets. A good next-generation enterprise planning solution will thus translate between financial and nonfinancial metrics (such as head count, materials, and product units).

  Enhanced creation and management of what-if models. What if we open additional regional facilities? What if interest rates rise dramatically? What if the sales department misses its quarterly goal by 10 percent? Modeling and assessing divergent business scenarios represent a big part of best practices planning. Spreadsheet-based systems, however, have made it difficult to work with multiple theoretical scenarios: They simply lack the tools required to relate the hypothetical scenarios in meaningful ways. In contrast, next-generation planning solutions make it possible to manage multiple alternative scenarios in a common manner, allowing decision-makers across the enterprise to freely experiment with various hypothetical conditions without creating document chaos or undermining the integrity of core planning documents.

## THE BENEFITS OF NEXT-GENERATION PLANNING SOLUTIONS

Next-generation planning technology derives its business value from the best practices it facilitates. The following subsections describe some of the key benefits companies experience with these technology-enabled planning best practices.

### Rapid Response to Change

When you reduce planning cycle times, you significantly improve your organization's ability to respond to change—whether those changes are in the buying habits of customers or in the state of the economy as a whole. Instead of being a problem, change becomes an opportunity that your organizations can use to achieve competitive advantage over less-nimble competitors.

### Actionable, Accessible Business Insight

When all planning data across the enterprise is available in a single, easy-to-navigate application, managers can effortlessly zoom up and drill down in search of data. This leads to better decisions being made more quickly, more confidently, and with greater consistency.

### Predictable Performance

Capital markets reward companies that consistently "make their numbers"; however, it's hard to achieve that consistency when planning cycles lag behind market conditions and your planning process includes substantial opportunity for error. Next-generation enterprise planning technology solves these problems by allowing you to continually assess real performance versus projected results, rigorously maintaining alignment between what-if predictions and execution.

### Optimal Resource Allocation

If marketing is planning a major push for Product A, the last thing you want to do is invest in increased manufacturing capacity for Product B. However, optimal resource allocation can only occur if planning is linked across all areas of your organization based on logical dependencies. With a unified enterprise planning environment in place, you can use such linkages to ensure that every dollar spent on infrastructure, payroll, materials, and outside services is optimally allocated.

## Full Participation of All Teams and Departments

Business is a team sport, which means that optimum bottom-line performance can only occur when everyone at every level and across every functional area is working together to achieve a common set of clearly understood goals. A shared enterprise planning environment that uses both financial and nonfinancial data ensures both the full enfranchisement of all appropriate process participants and the consistent enforcement of business priorities in every team, department, and business unit.

## Improved Vision and Leadership

No planning software can provide a crystal ball for managers; however, next- generation enterprise planning technology can make it much easier to examine and develop strategies for dealing with whatever the future holds. The ability to consider and experiment with a wide range of what-if scenarios greatly empowers managers at all levels. By providing them a clearer vision of the future, they and allowing them to exercise greater creativity in planning and to more aggressively pursue future opportunities.

These are just a few of the reasons it's imperative that businesses not remain complacent in their approaches to planning. Businesses that fail to drive planning practices and tools forward will remain bound by slow, stovepiped planning processes, finding it difficult to compete with more-nimble and unified organizations that are much better at leveraging their resources.

## TRANSFORMING THE PLANNING ENVIRONMENT

Even if you're relatively certain your organization will derive significant benefits from the implementation of a next-generation enterprise planning solution, you need to be certain that you can achieve those gains with a minimal amount of pain (in terms of effort, disruption, and cost). Keep in mind, however, that hundreds of organizations in a range of vertical markets have already made the transition, which means you're ahead of the competitive curve but far from the bleeding edge: plenty of pioneers and early adopters have already paved the way by implementing and proving the viability of these technologies.

If you are considering spearheading your organization's enterprise planning initiative, you should

- Focus on your company's biggest planning problems first. Although planning best practices provide invaluable direction, not every company has to implement every practice—or do so all at once. Often, it's wiser to focus on alleviating the most pressing planning issues first. Whether you want to achieve shorter cycle times or better alignment between marketing and sales, by attacking high-priority issues first, you can score big, easy wins early that help you gain the support and credibility required to continue the transition.
- Build broad-based consensus for change. Acquiring the right technology is key to improved enterprise planning, but to take full advantage of that technology, the entire organization needs to have a clear sense of (and commitment to) the goals of the planning initiative. In addition, initiative leaders will need to be given strong incentives to buy into and support the initiative as it impacts their areas of the organization.

- Make life as easy as possible for users. Because next-generation enterprise planning aims to promote broad involvement across an organization, end- user acceptance is critical, and every effort should be made to accommodate their needs. This means selecting an intuitive planning tool, providing all necessary training, and even allowing more change-averse constituencies to continue using spreadsheets as their primary desktop tool. Choose the right technology partner. The right partner can provide three essential ingredients in any successful enterprise planning initiative: superior technology, a mature understanding of corporate planning objectives, and experience in helping other organizations make the transition.

Two additional technical issues you" need to consider are how to migrate existing data in enterprise systems and how to integrate the solution with existing systems. You should also look for scalability, highly customizable planning workflow rules, and flexible calculation tools.

Although the challenges associated with overhauling an enterprise planning environment can seem daunting, they pale in comparison to the challenges associated with trying to succeed in today's supercompetitive business world without one. Companies must make planning decisions faster and with more intelligence and accuracy than ever before—and the only way they can do so is by putting in place next-generation enterprise planning technology.

## CHOOSING AN ENTERPRISE PLANNING SOLUTION

By combining prepackaged software with business intelligence capabilities and proven best planning practices, next-generation enterprise planning solutions optimize business planning across the enterprise. With the right enterprise planning technology in place, you will be able to drive collaborative, integrated event-based planning at all levels of your organization and with all appropriate participants.

When choosing an enterprise planning solution, you should verify that it covers the following functional areas:

- Strategic modeling. Your enterprise planning solution should allow you to analyze, evaluate, and choose strategic financial models; model balance sheets, income statements, and cash flows; and run different scenarios on margins and investment requirements.
- Financial planning and forecasting. The planning environment should allow you to create, track, and monitor business plans and forecasts in real time, and consolidate forecasts by geography and product.
- Operational planning. Your enterprise planning solution should speed workforce, capital, and project planning across the enterprise, providing real- time awareness of the impacts of your resource allocation decisions.

## CONCLUSION

A world-class enterprise planning solution represents a key component of any enterprise performance management system by bringing discipline to strategic financial modeling, facilitating enterprisewide operational planning and forecasting, and linking strategies with operations.

By letting management, finance, and operating staff focus on analyzing information rather than gathering and processing it, such solutions provide organizations with the agility they need to capitalize on business opportunities, optimize resources, and link strategic goals to operational plans.

7

# ADVANTAGES AND DISADVANTAGES OF FORMING A CORPORATION

A *corporation* is defined as a legal entity or structure created under the authority of a state's laws, consisting of a person or group of persons who become shareholders. The entity's existence is considered separate and distinct from that of its members. Like a real person, a corporation can enter into contracts, sue and be sued, pay taxes separately from its owners, and do the other things necessary to conduct business.

Incorporation can be a complicated process. You may choose to hire an attorney to guide you through the process (read Do I Need an Attorney to Form a Corporation? for more information).

Regardless of the tack you take, take into consideration the advantages and disadvantages listed below before you embark on incorporating your company. And when you're ready to incorporate, make sure to read Once You've Decided to Incorporate.

### *Advantages*

- Limited liability. One of the key reasons for forming a corporation is the limited liability protection provided to its owners. Because a corporation is considered a separate legal entity, the shareholders have limited liability for the corporation's debts. The personal assets of shareholders are not at risk for satisfying corporate debts or liabilities.

- Corporate tax treatment. Since a corporation is a separate legal entity, it pays taxes separate and apart from its owners (at least in the typical C corporation). Owners of a corporation only pay taxes on corporate profits paid to them in the form of salaries, bonuses, and dividends. The corporation pays taxes, at the corporate rate, on any profits.
- Attractive investment. The built-in stock structure of a corporation makes it attractive to investors.
- Capital incentive. The stock structure also allows corporations to attract key and talented employees by offering them an ownership interest in the form of stock options or stock.
- Owner/employee. A business owner who works in his or her own business may become an employee and thus be eligible for reimbursement or deduction of many types of expenses, including health and life insurance.
- Operational structure. Corporations have a set management structure. The owners of a corporation are shareholders, who elect a Board of Directors, which then elects the officers. Other than the election of directors, shareholders do not participate in the operations of the corporation. The Board of Directors is responsible for managing and exercising the rights and responsibilities of the corporation. The Board sets corporate policy and the strategy for the corporation, and elects officers — usually a CEO, vice president, treasurer, and secretary — to follow

the policies set by the Board, and manage the corporation on a day-to-day basis. In a small corporation, the lines between the shareholders, Board of Directors, and officers tends to blur because the same people may be serving in all capacities.

- Perpetual existence. A corporation continues to exist until the shareholders decide to dissolve it or merge with another business.
- Freely transferable shares. Shares of corporations are freely transferable, because as a separate entity, the existence of a corporation is not dependent upon who the owners or investors are at any one time. A corporation continues to exist as a separate entity, and is not terminated or dissolved even when shareholders die or sell their shares. Shares of corporations are freely transferable unless shareholders have "buy-sell" agreements limiting when and to whom shares may be sold or transferred. Also, securities laws may restrict the transferability of shares.

### *Disadvantages*

- Fees. It costs money to incorporate. There are four types of fees: a fee to file the Articles of Incorporation with the Secretary of State, a first-year franchise tax prepayment, fees for various governmental filings, and attorneys' fees. But every year, tens of thousands of businesses choose to incorporate online without the use of an attorney.
- Formalities. The proper corporate formalities of organizing and running a corporation must be followed, to receive the benefits of being a corporation.
- Paperwork. Paperwork is a huge component of the corporate formalities that must followed. Reports

and tax returns must be compiled and filed in a timely fashion; business bank accounts and records must be maintained and kept separate from personal accounts and assets; records must be kept of corporate actions, including meetings of shareholders and Board of Directors; and licenses must be maintained.

- Disclosure of names of corporate officers and directors. Most states do not require that names of shareholders be a matter of public record; however, many states require that the names and addresses of corporate officers and directors be listed on one or more documents filed with the Secretary of State.
- Dissolution. Since corporations have a perpetual existence, states provide a mechanism for dissolving a corporation and liquidating its assets. Dissolution does not happen automatically. A corporation can be dissolved voluntarily or involuntarily. A corporation's officers and directors are charged with responsibility for dissolving the corporation, including gathering corporate assets, paying creditors and outstanding claims, and distributing the remaining assets to shareholders.
- Tax consequences. C corporations have potential double-tax consequences — once when the company makes its profit, and a second time when dividends are paid to shareholders. S corporations can mitigate this tax issue.

## BUSINESS PLAN FOR AN ESTABLISHED BUSINESS

This business plan consists of a narrative and several financial spreadsheets. The narrative template is the body of the business plan. It contains more than 150 questions divided into several sections. Work through the sections in any order you like, except for the *Executive Summary*, which should be done last. Skip any questions that do not apply to your business. When you are finished writing your first draft, you will have a collection of small essays on the various topics of the business plan. Then you will want to edit them into a flowing narrative. The real value of doing a business plan is not having the finished product in hand; rather, the value lies in the process of research and thinking about your business in a systematic way. The act of planning helps you to think things through thoroughly, to study and research when you are not sure of the facts, and to look at your ideas critically. It takes time, but avoids costly, perhaps disastrous, mistakes later.

The business plan narrative is a generic model suitable for all types of businesses. However, you should modify it to suit your particular circumstances. Before you begin, review the section titled *Refining the Plan*, found at the end of the business plan. It suggests emphasizing certain areas, depending upon your type of business (manufacturing, retail, service, etc.). It also has tips for fine-tuning your plan to make an effective presentation to investors or bankers. If this is why you are writing your plan, pay particular attention to your writing style. You will be judged by the quality and appearance of your work as well as your ideas.

It typically takes several weeks to complete a good plan. Most of that time is spent in research and rethinking your ideas and assumptions. But then, that is the value of the process. So make time to do the job properly. Those who do never regret the effort. And finally, be sure to keep detailed notes on your sources of information and on the assumptions underlying your financial data.

## Business Plan

**Mission Statement:** Many companies have a brief mission statement, usually 30 words or fewer, explaining their reason for being and their guiding principles. If you have a mission statement, this is a good place to put it in the plan, followed by company goals and objectives and business philosophy.

What business are you in? What do you do?

What is your target market? (Explain briefly here, because you will do a more thorough explanation in the *Marketing Plan* section.)

Describe your Industry. Is it a growth industry? What changes do you foresee in your industry, and how is your company poised to take advantage of them?

Now give a detailed description of the business:

**Form of Ownership:** Sole proprietor, partnership, corporation, or limited liability corporation (LLC)?

**Company History:** Years in business, previous owners, successes, failures, lessons learned, reputation in community, sales and profit history, number of employees, and events that affected success. Discuss significant past problems and how you solved and survived them.

Most important strengths and core competencies: What factors will make the company succeed? What are your major competitive strengths? What strengths do you personally bring to the business?

Significant challenges the company faces now and in the near future: If you are asking for funding, go on to explain how the new capital will help you meet these challenges.

**Long Term:** What are your plans for the future of the business? Growth? If so, at what rate and how will you achieve it?

Are you developing strategies for continued growth, increased production, diversification, or eventual sale of the business? What are your time frames for these?

### Products and Services

Describe in depth your products and services. (Technical specifications, drawings, photos, sales brochures, and other bulky items belong in the *Appendices.*)

What factors give you competitive advantages or disadvantages? For example, the level of quality, or unique or proprietary features.

What is the pricing, fee, or leasing structure of your products and services?

### Market Research: Why?

You spend so much time on marketing-related matters— customers, competitors, pricing, promotion, and advertising— that it is natural to assume that you have little to learn. However, every small business can benefit from doing market research to make sure it is on track. Use the business planning process as your opportunity to uncover data and to question your marketing efforts. It will be time well spent.

#### *Market Research: How?*

There are two kinds of market research: primary and secondary.

Secondary research means using published information such as industry profiles, trade journals, newspapers, magazines, census data, and demographic profiles. This type of information is available from public libraries, industry associations, chambers of commerce, vendors who sell to your industry, and government agencies.

Start with your local library. Most librarians are pleased to guide you through their business data collection. You will be amazed at what is there. There are more online sources than you could possibly use. Your chamber of commerce has good information on the local area. Trade associations and trade publications often have excellent industry-specific data.

Primary market research means gathering your own data. For example, you could do your own traffic count at a proposed location, use the yellow pages to identify competitors, and do surveys or focus group interviews to learn about consumer preferences. Professional market research can be very costly, but there are many books that show small business owners how to do effective research.

In your marketing plan, be as specific as possible; give statistics, numbers, and sources. The marketing plan will be the basis, later on, of the all-important sales projection.

### *The Marketing Plan: Economics*

- Facts about your industry
- Total size of your market
- Percentage share of the market you have. (This is important only if you are a major factor in the market.)
- Current demand in target market
- Growth history
- Trends in target market — growth trends, trends in consumer preferences, and trends in product development
- Growth potential and opportunity for a business of your size
- What barriers to entry keep potential new competitors from flooding into your market?
    - High capital costs
    - High production costs
    - High marketing costs
    - Consumer acceptance/brand recognition
    - Training/skills

  - * Unique technology/patents
  - * Unions
  - * Shipping costs
  - * Tariff barriers/quotas
- How could the following affect your company?
  - * Change in technology
  - * Government regulations
  - * Changing economy
  - * Change in your industry

### *Products*

In the *Products and Services* section, you described your products and services as you see them. Now describe them from your customers' point of view.

#### Features and Benefits

List all your major products or services.

For each product or service, describe the most important features. That is, what does the product do? What is special about it?

Now, for each product or service, describe its benefits. That is, what does the product do for the customer?

Note the differences between features and benefits, and think about them. For example, a house gives shelter and lasts a long time; those are its features. Its benefits include pride of ownership, financial security, providing for the family, and inclusion in a neighborhood. You build features into your product so you can sell the benefits.

What after-sale services are supplied? For example: delivery, warranty, service contracts, support, follow-up, or refund policy.

### *Customers*

Identify your customers, their characteristics, and their geographic locations; that is, demographics.

The description will be completely different depending on whether you sell to other businesses or directly to consumers. If you sell a consumer product, but sell it through a channel of distributors, wholesalers, and retailers, you must carefully analyze both the end user and the intermediary businesses to which you sell.

You may have more than one customer group. Identify the most important groups. Then, for each consumer group, construct a demographic profile:

*Age*

*Gender*

*Location*

*Income level*

*Social class/occupation*

*Education*

*Other*

For business customers, the demographic factors might be:

*Industry (or portion of an industry)*

*Location*

*Size of firm*

*Quality/technology/price preferences*

*Other*

### *Competition*

What products and companies compete with you? List your major competitors, including their names and addresses.

Do they compete with you across the board, just for certain products, certain customers, or in certain locations?

Use the following table to compare your company with your three most important competitors.

In the first column are key competitive factors. Because these vary with each market, you may want to customize the list of factors.

***Table: Competitive Analysis***

| FACTOR | Me | Strength | Weakness | Competitor A | Competitor B | Competitor C | Importance to customer |
|---|---|---|---|---|---|---|---|
| Products | | | | | | | |
| Price | | | | | | | |
| Quality | | | | | | | |
| Selection | | | | | | | |
| Service | | | | | | | |
| Reliability | | | | | | | |
| Stability | | | | | | | |
| Expertise | | | | | | | |
| Company reputation | | | | | | | |
| Location | | | | | | | |
| Appearance | | | | | | | |
| Sales method | | | | | | | |
| Credit policies | | | | | | | |
| Advertising | | | | | | | |
| Image | | | | | | | |

In the cell labeled "Me," state honestly how you think you stack up in customers' minds. Then decide whether you think this factor is a strength or a weakness for you. If you find it hard to analyze yourself this way, enlist some disinterested party to assess you. This can be a real eye-opener.

Now analyze each major competitor. In a few words, state how you think they stack up.

In the last column, estimate how important each competitive factor is to the customer. 1 = critical; 5 = not very important.

After you finish the competitive matrix, write a short paragraph stating your competitive advantages and disadvantages.

### *Niche*

Now that you have systematically analyzed your industry, your product, your customers, and the competition, you should have a clear picture of where your company fits into the world.

In one short paragraph, define your niche, your unique corner of the market.

### *Marketing Strategy*

Now outline a marketing strategy that is consistent with your niche.

Promotion: How do you get the word out to customers?

Advertising: What media do you use, why, and how often? Has your advertising been effective? How can you tell?

Do you use other methods, such as trade shows, catalogs, dealer incentives, word of mouth, and network of friends or professionals?

If you have identifiable repeat customers, do you have a systematic contact plan?

Why this mix and not some other?

### *Promotional Budget*

How much will you spend on the items listed above?

Should you consider spending less on some promotional activities and more on others?

### *Pricing*

What is your pricing strategy? For most small businesses, having the lowest prices is not a good strategy. Usually you will do better to have average prices and compete on quality and service. Does your pricing strategy fit with what was revealed in your competitive analysis?

Compare your prices with those of your competition. Are they higher, lower, the same? Why?

How important is price as a competitive factor?

What are your payment and customer credit policies?

### *Location*

You will describe your physical location in the *Operational Plan* section of your business plan. Here in the *Marketing Plan* section, analyze your location as it affects your customers.

If customers come to your place of business:

Is it convenient? Parking? Interior spaces? Not out of the way?

Is it consistent with your image?

Is it what customers want and expect?

Where is the competition located? Is it better for you to be near them (like car dealers or fast-food restaurants) or distant (like convenience food stores)?

### *Distribution Channels*

How do you sell your products or services?

- Retail
- Direct (mail order, World Wide Web, catalog)
- Wholesale
- Your own sales force
- Agents
- Independent reps

Has your marketing strategy proven effective?

Do you need to make any changes or additions to current strategies?

### *Sales Forecast*

Now that you have described your products, services, customers, markets, and marketing plans in detail, it is time to attach some numbers to your plan. Use a forecast spreadsheet to prepare a month-by-month projection. Base the forecast on your historical sales, the marketing strategies that you have just described, your market research, and industry data, if available.

You may want to do two forecasts: 1) a "best guess," which is what you really expect, and 2) a "worst case" low estimate that you are confident you can reach no matter what happens.

Remember to keep notes on your research and your assumptions as you build this sales forecast and all subsequent spreadsheets in the plan. Relate the forecast to your sales history, explaining the major differences between past and projected sales. This is critical if you are going to present it to funding sources.

## Operational Plan

Explain the daily operation of the business, its location, equipment, people, processes, and surrounding environment.

### *Production*

How and where do you produce your products or services?

Explain your methods of:

Production techniques and costs

Quality control

Customer service

Inventory control

Product development

### *Location*

Describe the locations of production, sales, storage areas, and buildings.

Do you lease or own your premises?

Describe access to your buildings (walk in, parking, freeway, airport, railroad, and shipping).

What are your business hours?

If you are trying to get an expansion loan, include a drawing or layout of your proposed facility.

### *Legal Environment*

Describe the following:

Licensing and bonding requirements

Permits

Health, workplace, or environmental regulations

Special regulations covering your industry or profession

Zoning or building code requirements

Insurance coverage

Trademarks, copyrights, or patents (pending, existing, or purchased)

***Personnel***

Number of employees

Type of labor (skilled, unskilled, professional)

Where do you find new employees?

Quality of existing staff

Pay structure

Training methods and requirements

New hiring in the coming year?

Who does which tasks?

Are schedules and procedures in place?

Do you have written job descriptions for employees? If not, take time to write some. Written job descriptions really help internal communications with employees.

Do you use contract workers as well as employees?

***Inventory***

What kind of inventory do you keep: raw materials, supplies, finished goods?

Average value in stock; that is, what is your inventory investment?

Rate of turnover and how it compares with industry averages?

Seasonal buildups?

Lead time for ordering?

***Suppliers***

Note the following information about your suppliers:

Their names and addresses.

Type and amount of inventory furnished.

Credit and delivery policies.

History and reliability.

Do you expect shortages or short-term delivery problems?

Are supply costs steady or fluctuating? If fluctuating, how do you deal with changing costs?

Should you be searching out new sources of supply, or are you satisfied with present suppliers?

### *Credit Policies*

Do you sell on credit? If so, do you really need to? Is it customary in your industry and expected by your clientele?

Do you carefully monitor your payables (what you owe to vendors) to take advantage of discounts and to keep your credit rating good?

You need to carefully manage both the credit you extend and the credit you receive.

### *Managing Your Accounts Receivable*

If you do extend credit, what are your policies about who gets credit and how much?

How do you check the creditworthiness of new applicants?

What terms will you offer your customers; that is, how much credit and when is payment due?

Do you offer prompt payment discounts? (It is best to do this only if it is usual and customary in your industry.)

Do you know what it costs you to extend credit? This includes both the cost of capital tied up in receivables and the cost of bad debts.

Have you built the costs into your prices?

You should do an aging at least monthly to track how much of your money is tied up in credit given to customers and to alert you to slow payment problems. A receivables aging looks like the following table.

*Table: Accounts Receivable Aging*

| | Total | Current | 30 Days | 60 Days | 90 Days | Over 90 Days |
|---|---|---|---|---|---|---|
| ınts receivable | | | | | | |
| | | | | | | |

Collecting from delinquent customers is no fun. You need a set policy and you need to follow it.

When do you make a phone call?

When do you send a letter?

When do you get your attorney to threaten?

### *Managing Your Accounts Payable*

You should also age your accounts payable (what you owe to your suppliers). Use this format.

*Table 3: Accounts Payable Aging*

| | Total | Current | 30 Days | 60 Days | 90 Days | Over 90 Days |
|---|---|---|---|---|---|---|
| Accounts payable aging | | | | | | |
| | | | | | | |

This helps you plan whom to pay and when. Paying too early depletes your cash, but paying late can cost you valuable discounts and damage your credit. (Hint: If you know you will be late making a payment, call the creditor before the due date. It tends to relax them.)

Are prompt payment discounts offered by your proposed vendors? Do you always take them?

## MANAGEMENT AND ORGANIZATION

Who manages the business on a day-to-day basis?

What experience does that person bring to the business? What special or distinctive competencies?

Is there a plan for continuation of the business if this person is lost or incapacitated?

If you have more than 10 employees, prepare an organizational chart showing the management hierarchy and who is responsible for key functions. Include position descriptions for key employees.

### Professional and Advisory Support

List the following:

Board of directors and management advisory board

Attorney

Accountant

Insurance agent

Banker

Consultants

Mentors and key advisors

### Personal Financial Statement

Owners often have to draw on personal assets to finance the business. This statement will show you what is available. Bankers and investors usually want this information as well. They will ask owners to cosign or personally guarantee any business loans.

Document your assumptions, notes, definitions, and any special financial situation. Include details of notes, securities, contracts, etc. on the bottom of a personal financial spreadsheet. Include one such spreadsheet for each principal.

## Financial History and Analysis

A solid analysis of the past must precede any serious attempt to forecast the future. A financial history and ratios spreadsheet will allow you to put a great deal of financial information from other statements on a single page for ease of comprehension and analysis. You may also enter industry average ratios for comparison. In the *Appendices*, put year-end balance sheets, operating statements, and business income tax returns for the past three years, plus your most current balance sheet and operating statement.

### *Debt Schedule*

This table gives in-depth information that the financial statements themselves do not usually provide. Include a debt schedule in the following format for each note payable on your most recent balance sheet.

***Table: Debt Schedule***

| To whom payable | Original amount | Original date | Present balance | Rate of interest | Maturity date | Monthly payment | Security | Current/ past due |
|---|---|---|---|---|---|---|---|---|
| | | | | | | | | |
| | | | | | | | | |

## FINANCIAL PLAN

The financial plan consists of a 12-month profit and loss projection, a four-year profit and loss projection (optional), a cash-flow projection, a projected balance sheet, and a breakeven calculation.

Together, these spreadsheets constitute a reasonable estimate of your company's financial future. More important, however, the process of thinking through the financial plan will improve your insight into the inner financial workings of your company.

### *12-Month Profit and Loss Projection*

Explain the major assumptions used to estimate company income and expenses. Your sales projection should come from an annual sales forecast. Pay special attention to areas where historical performance varies markedly from your projections.

### *Four-Year Profit Projection (Optional)*

The 12-month projection is the heart of your financial plan. However, this worksheet is for those who want to carry their forecasts beyond the first year. It is expected of those seeking venture capital. Bankers pay more attention to the 12-month projection.

Of course, keep notes of your key assumptions, especially about things you expect to change dramatically over the years.

### *Projected Cash Flow*

The cash-flow projection is just a forward look at your checking account.

For each item, determine when you actually expect to receive cash (for sales) or when you will actually have to write a check (for expense items).

Your cash flow will show you whether your working capital is adequate. Clearly if your cash on hand goes negative, you will need more. It will also show when and how much you need to borrow.

Explain your major assumptions, especially those that make the cash flow differ from a profit and loss statement, such as:

If you make a sale in month 1, when do you actually collect the cash? When you buy inventory or materials, do you pay in advance, upon delivery, or much later?

How will this affect cash flow?

Are some expenses payable in advance?

Are there irregular expenses, equipment purchase, or inventory buildup that should be budgeted?

And of course, depreciation does not appear at all because you never write a check for it.

### *Projected Balance Sheet*

This is an estimate of what the balance sheet will look like at the end of the 12-month period covered in your projections. In the business plan section related to your projected balance sheet, state the assumptions that you used for all major changes between your last historical balance sheet and the projection.

### *Breakeven Analysis*

A breakeven analysis determines the sales volume, at a given price, that is required to recover total costs.

Expressed as a formula, breakeven is as follows.

$$\text{Breakeven sales} = \frac{\text{Fixed costs}}{1- \text{Variable costs}}$$

(Where fixed costs are expressed in dollars, but variable costs are expressed as a percentage of total sales.)

### *Appendices*

Include details and studies used in your business plan; for example:

Brochures and advertising materials

Industry studies

Blueprints and plans

Maps and photos of location

Magazine or other articles

Detailed lists of equipment owned or to be purchased

Copies of leases and contracts

Letters of support from future customers

Any other materials needed to support the assumptions in this plan

Market research studies

## Refining the Plan

The generic business plan presented above should be modified to suit your specific type of business and the audience for which the plan is written.

## For Raising Capital

### *For Bankers*

Bankers want assurance of orderly repayment. If you intend to use this plan to present to lenders, include:

Amount of loan.

How you will use the funds.

What will this accomplish (how will it make the business stronger)?

Requested repayment terms (number of years to repay). You will probably not have much negotiating room on interest rate, but you may be able to negotiate a longer repayment term, which will help cash flow.

Collateral offered, and a list of all existing liens against the collateral.

### *For Investors*

Investors have a different perspective from bankers. They are looking for dramatic growth, and they expect to share in the rewards. Include the following in the plan that you present to potential investors:

**Funds Needed Short Term**

Funds needed in two to five years

How the company will use the funds, and what this will accomplish for growth

Estimated return on investment

Exit strategy for investors (buyback, sale, or IPO)

Percentage of ownership that you will give up to investors

Milestones or conditions that you will accept

Financial reporting that you will provide

Involvement of investors on the board or in management

**Refine Your Plan for the Type of Business**

***Manufacturing***

Present production levels

Present levels of direct production costs and indirect (overhead) costs

Gross profit margin, overall and for each product line

Possible production efficiency increases

Production-capacity limits of existing physical plant

Production capacity of expanded plant (if expansion is planned)

Production-capacity limits of existing equipment

Production capacity of new equipment (if new equipment is planned)

Prices per product line

Purchasing and inventory management procedures

Anticipated modifications or improvements to existing products

New products under development or anticipated

### *Service Businesses*

Service businesses sell intangible products. They are usually more flexible than other types of business, but they also have higher labor costs and generally very little in fixed assets.

Prices

Methods used to set prices

System of production management

Quality control procedures

Standard or accepted industry quality standards

How do you measure labor productivity?

What percentage of total available hours do you bill to customers?

Breakeven billable hours

Percentage of work subcontracted to other firms

Profit on subcontracting?

Credit, payment, and collections policies and procedures

Strategy for keeping client base

Strategy for attracting new clients

### *High-Tech Companies*

Economic outlook for the industry

Does your company have information systems in place to manage rapidly changing prices, costs, and markets?

Is your company on the cutting edge with its products and services?

What is the status of R&D? And what is required to bring the product or service to market and to keep the company competitive?

How does the company:

Protect intellectual property?

Avoid technological obsolescence?

Supply necessary capital?

Retain key personnel?

If your company is not yet profitable or perhaps does not yet even have sales, you must do longer-term financial forecasts to show when profit take-off will occur. And your assumptions must be well documented and well argued.

***Retail Business***

- Company image
- Pricing: Explain mark-up policies. Prices should be profitable, competitive, and in accord with the company image.
- Inventory:
- Selection and price should be consistent with company image.
- Calculate your annual inventory turnover rate. Compare this to the industry average for your type of store.
- Customer service policies: These should be competitive and in accord with the company image.
- Location: Does it give the exposure you need? Is it convenient for customers? Is it consistent with company image?
- Promotion: What methods do you use and what do they cost? Do they project a consistent company image?

- Credit: Do you extend credit to customers? If yes, do you really need to, and do you factor the cost into prices?

Financial management in the small firm is characterized, in many different cases, by the need to confront a somewhat different set of problems and opportunities than those confronted by a large corporation. One immediate and obvious difference is that a majority of smaller firms do not normally have the opportunity to publicly sell issues of stocks or bonds in order to raise funds. The owner-manager of a smaller firm must rely primarily on trade credit, bank financing, lease financing, and personal equity to finance the business. One, therefore faces a much more severely restricted set of financing alternatives than those faced by the financial vice president or treasurer of a large corporation.

On the other hand, many financial problems facing the small firm are very similar to those of larger corporations. For example, the analysis required for a long-term investment decision such as the purchase of heavy machinery or the evaluation of lease-buy alternatives, is essentially the same regardless of the size of the firm. Once the decision is made, the financing alternatives available to the firm may be radically different, but the decision process will be generally similar.

One area of particular concern for the smaller business owner lies in the effective management of working capital. Net working capital is defined as the difference between current assets and current liabilities and is often thought of as the "circulating capital" of the business. Lack of control in this crucial area is a primary cause of business failure in both small and large firms.

The business manager must continually be alert to changes in working capital accounts, the cause of these changes and the implications of these changes for the financial health of the company. One convenient and effective method to highlight the key managerial requirements in this area is to view working capital in terms of its major components:

### *Cash and Equivalents*

This most liquid form of current assets, cash and cash equivalents (usually marketable securities or short-term certificate of deposit) requires constant supervision. A well planned and maintained cash budgeting system is essential to answer key questions such as: Is the cash level adequate to meet current expenses as they come due?

What are the timing relationships between cash inflows and outflows? When will peak cash needs occur? What will be the magnitude of bank borrowing required to meet any cash shortfalls? When will this borrowing be necessary and when may repayment be expected?

### *Accounts Receivable*

Almost all businesses are required to extend credit to their customers. Key issues in this area include: Is the amount of accounts receivable reasonable in relation to sales? On the average, how rapidly are accounts receivable being collected? Which customers are "slow payers?" What action should be taken to speed collections where needed?

### *Inventories*

Inventories often make up 50 percent or more of a firm's current assets and therefore, are deserving of close scrutiny.

Key questions which must be considered in this area include: Is the level of inventory reasonable in relation to sales and the operating characteristics of the business? How rapidly is inventory turned over in relation to other companies in the same industry? Is any capital invested in dead or slow moving stock? Are sales being lost due to inadequate inventory levels? If appropriate, what action should be taken to increase or decrease inventory?

### *Accounts Payable and Trade Notes Payable*

In a business, trade credit often provides a major source of financing for the firm. Key issues to investigate in this category include: Is the amount of money owed to suppliers reasonable in relation to purchases? Is the firm's payment policy such that it will enhance or detract from the firm's credit rating? If available, are discounts being taken? What are the timing relationships between payments on accounts payable and collection on accounts receivable?

### *Notes Payable*

Notes payable to banks or other lenders are a second major source of financing for the business. Important questions in this class include: What is the amount of bank borrowing employed? Is this debt amount reasonable in relation to the equity financing of the firm? When will principal and interest payments fall due? Will funds be available to meet these payments on time?

### *Accrued Expenses and Taxes Payable*

Accrued expenses and taxes payable represent obligations of the firm as of the date of balance sheet preparation.

Accrued expenses represent such items as salaries payable, interest payable on bank notes, insurance premiums payable, and similar items. Of primary concern in this area, particularly with regard to taxes payable, is the magnitude, timing, and availability of funds for payment. Careful planning is required to insure that these obligations are met on time.

As a final note, it is important to recognize that although the working capital accounts above are listed separately, they must also be viewed in total and from the point of view of their relationship to one another: What is the overall trend in net working capital?

Is this a healthy trend? Which individual accounts are responsible for the trend? How does the firm's working capital position relate to similar sized firms in the industry? What can be done to correct the trend, if necessary?

Of course, the questions posed are much easier to ask than to answer and there are few "general" answers to the issues raised. The guides which follow provide suggestions, techniques, and guidelines for successful management which, when tempered with the experience of the individual owner-manager and the unique requirements of the particular industry, may be expected to enhance one's ability to effectively manage the financial resources of a business enterprise.

## What is the Business Plan?

The business plan sets out how the owners/managers of a business intend to realise its objectives. Without such a plan a business is likely to drift.

The business plan serves several purposes:it

(1) enables management to think through the business in a logical and structured way and to set out the stages in the achievement of the business objectives.

(2) enables management to plot progress against the plan (through the management accounts)

(3) ensures that both the resources needed to carry out the strategy and the time when they are required are identified.

(4) is a means for making all employees aware of the business's direction (assuming the key features of the business plan are communicated to employees)

(5) is an important document for for discussion with prospective investors and lenders of finance (e.g. banks and venture capitalists).

(6) links into the detailed, short-term, one-year budget.

## The Link Between the Business Plan and the Budget

A budget can be defined as "a financial or quantitative statement", prepared for a specific accounting period (typically a year), containing the plans and policies to be pursued during that period.

The main purposes of a budget are:

(1) to monitor business unit and managerial performance (the latter possibly linking into bonus arrangements)

(2) to forecast the out-turn of the period's trading (through the use of flexed budgets and based on variance analyses)

(3) to assist with cost control.

Generally, a functional budget is prepared for each functional area within a business (e.g. call-centre, marketing, production, research and development, finance and administration). In addition, it is also normal to produce a "capital budget" detailing the capital investment required for the period, a "cash flow budget", a "stock budget" and a "master budget", which includes the budgeted profit and loss account and balance sheet.

## Preparing a Business Plan

A business plan has to be particular to the organisation in question, its situation and time. However, a business plan is not just a document, to be produced and filed.

Business planning is a continuous process. The business plan has to be a living document, constantly in use to monitor, control and guide the progress of a business. That means it should be under regular review and will need to be amended in line with changing circumstances.

Before preparing the plan management should:

- review previous business plans (if any) and their outcome. This review will help highlight which areas of the business have proved difficult to forecast historically. For example, are sales difficult to estimate? If so why?
- be very clear as to their objectives - a business plan must have a purpose
- set out the key business assumptions on which their plans will be based (e.g. inflation, exchange rates, market growth, competitive pressures, etc.)
- take a critical look at their business. The classical way is by means of the strengths-weaknesses-opportunities-threats (SWOT) analysis, which identifies the business's situation from four key angles. The strategies adopted by a business will be largely based on the outcome of this analysis.

## Preparing the Budget

A typical business plan looks up to three years forward and it is normal for the first year of the plan to be set out in considerable detail. This one-year plan, or budget, will be prepared in such a way that progress can be regularly monitored (usually monthly) by checking the variance between the actual performance and the budget, which will be phased to take account of seasonal variations.

The budget will show financial figures (cash, profit/loss working capital, etc) and also non-financial items such as personnel numbers, output, order book, etc. Budgets can be produced for units, departments and products as well as for the total organisation.

Budgets for the forthcoming period are usually produced before the end of the current period. While it is not usual for budgets to be changed during the period to which they relate (apart from the most extraordinary circumstances) it is common practice for revised forecasts to be produced during the year as circumstances change.

A further refinement is to flex the budgets, i.e. to show performance at different levels of business. This makes comparisons with actual outcomes more meaningful in cases where activity levels differ from those included in the budget.

## What Providers of Finance Want from a Business Plan

Almost invariably bank managers and other providers of finance will want to see a business plan before agreeing to provide finance. Not to have a business plan will be regarded as a bad sign.

They will be looking not only at the plan, but at the persons behind it. They will want details of the owner/managers of the business, their background and experience, other activities, etc. They will be looking for management commitment, with enthusiasm tempered by realism. The plan must be thought through and not be a skimpy piece of work. A few figures on a spreadsheet are not enough.

The plan must be used to run the business and there must be a means for checking progress against the plan. An information system must be in place to provide regular details of progress against plan.

Bank managers are particularly wary of businesses that are slow in producing internal performance figures. Lenders will want to guard against risk. In particular they will be looking for two assurances:

(1) that the business has the means of making regular payment of interest on the amount loaned, and

(2) that if everything goes wrong the bank can still get its money back (i.e. by having a debenture over the business's assets). Forward-looking financial statements, particularly the cash flow forecast, are therefore of critical importance. The bank wants openness and no surprises. If something is going wrong it does not want this covered up, it wants to be informed - quickly.

# 8

# BUSINESS FINANCIAL STATEMENTS

In this chapter, we build on the basic knowledge of how businesses are financed by looking at how firms organize and report financial information. This understanding of financial statements relates to economic development finance in several ways. First, it is critical for assisting individual businesses to secure financing. A careful reading of a firm's financial statements reveals how it has financed its activities and helps identify the appropriate financing to address its fiscal needs. Second, financial statement analysis is central to evaluating a firm's capacity to repay debt or generate the return required by equity investors. Third, financial statements provide insight into common financing issues faced by similar firms, such as those in the same industry, at the same stage of development, with similar ownership, or in the same size class. For all these reasons, development finance practitioners need to be literate with financial statements.

To develop this literacy, this chapter covers three topics. It begins by introducing several important concepts that underlie accounting and financial statements and explains the difference between accrual and cash accounting. Next, it explains the three major financial statements used to summarize businesses, the balance sheet, the income statement, and the cash flow statement and defines the major categories of financial information included on these reports. Future chapters build on this knowledge of financial statements to develop skills in evaluating a business's capacity to support new capital and in structuring appropriate financing.

Robert N. Anthony, David F. Hawkins, and Kenneth A. Merchant in their classic introduction to accounting, *Accounting: Text and Cases,* identify 11 basic concepts that guide accounting practice.1 While all eleven concepts are important, three concepts are especially helpful in highlighting how financial statements are prepared and clarifying the nature of accrual accounting. The first principal is called the *dual aspect concept,* which is summarized by a simple equation that is the foundation for the balance sheet.

This equation, assets = equities, indicates that everything that is owned by a firm (its assets) is claimed by someone, either its creditors (whose claims are called liabilities) or its owners (whose claims are called owner's equity). This concept is common sense; all of a firm's possessions must belong to someone. As discussed in the previous chapters, creditors have a first claim on a firm's assets while the owners have a residual claim.

An important corollary to the dual aspect concept is that every financial transaction of a business must impact at least two accounts of the firm. For the dual aspect equation to remain true, when a transaction increases an asset account, then either another asset account must decrease or an equity account must increase. Accountants use a system of debits and credits to keep the asset and equity aspects of a firm's financial accounts in balance. For every transaction, the total of debit entries must equal the total of credit entries to ensure that assets will equal equities after the transaction is recorded. Accounting is referred to as a dual entry record-keeping system due to the balancing of debits and credits for each transaction.

Two additional concepts, the realization concept and matching concept, are used to determine when revenue and expenses are recognized (i.e., recorded as such in the firm's accounts). Under the *realization concept,* revenue is recognized and credited to a firm's accounts when goods are shipped or services are rendered. Note that revenue is not recognized when payment is made for the goods or services. This is central to accrual accounting in which revenue is recorded when it is earned (i.e., when goods or services are provided), not when payment is received. Under the *matching concept,* which governs how expenses are allocated, expenses are recognized in the same period when the revenues associated with those costs are recorded. By matching expenses with the recognized revenue for a given period, financial statements provide an accurate representation of the economic results of the sales occurring during the period. Note, as with revenue, that expenses are not recorded based on when payment is made. Since some costs are not directly related to producing goods or services but are general costs of the firm (e.g., insurance or salaries for the accounting staff), these expenses are recognized in the period for which they are associated. Insurance costs and accounting department salaries for October would be recorded as an expense in the October accounting records.

The realization and matching concepts are central to accrual basis accounting, which is required under generally accepted accounting principals (GAAP), the standards for all private sector financial statements. To understand accrual accounting, it is helpful to compare it to cash basis financial reporting. Under cash basis reporting, transactions are recorded based on the receipt and expenditure of cash. Cash basis revenue is recorded when the payment for goods and services is received and expenses are recognized when cash payments are made. Cash basis reporting presents the impact of business activities on a firm's cash flow and cash position, but it has a serious pitfall. With cash basis financial reports, the income received during a period is not linked with the associated costs, and there is no determination of whether the business was profitable during a given time period.

Accrual accounting, on the other hand, does not follow the cash. Instead, it seeks to accurately present a firm's "earned income," the actual economic results of its activities over a period. Accrual accounting statements answer the question: What were a business's financial results for a period based on the revenue generated and the associated costs in that period, independent of when payment is received and bills are paid.

In differentiating accrual from cash accounting, it is useful to distinguish between *revenue,* the accrual concept, and *receipt,* the cash activity. Revenue refers to income generated by the provision of goods or services to a customer. Revenue is a function of the delivery of goods and services in a period, and its financial reporting is unrelated to the timing of any payment. Receipt refers to the collection of cash: it records when a customer makes a payment, which may differ from when the customer actually receives goods or services. A similar distinction exists between *expense,* the accrual concept, and *expenditure,* the cash transaction. Expenses refer to the costs incurred during a period that are related to either the generation of revenue in that period or a general business cost for the period. Expenses are recorded in financial statements independent of any cash outlays for the period.

Expenditure, on the other hand, refers to the outlay of cash, whether or not that outlay is tied to revenue-generating activities during that period. To see the difference in financial reports based on cash and accrual accounting, consider the following activities of College Books, a mail order bookstore during the month of September 2002. During this month, College Books shipped $2,000 in books to customers. These customers paid for the books in October, after their receipt. College Books acquired the inventory of books sold in September during the months of June, July, and August, paying $1,200 over these 3 months. General business costs for College Books are monthly rent payments of $200 paid on the first day of each month and monthly salaries of $500, paid on the last day of each month.

In the cash basis statement, no revenue is recorded in September since College Books did not receive any payment in this month. Similarly, no deduction is made for the cost of the books shipped in September since the firm paid for these books in the prior 3 months. The only cash payments in September were $700 for its rent and salaries.

Consequently, the cash basis statement for College Books shows a loss of $700. The accrual income statement reports income of $2,000 corresponding to the sales price for the books shipped that month. The cost of these books is matched to the revenue and reported as a $1,200 expense. The other $700 in monthly costs also are deducted as September expenses, showing a final net income of $100. Although the cash statement shows that College Books's bank account declined by $700 during September, it does not show the economic results of College Books's activities for the month (i.e., whether or not the firm earned a profit from its September sales). The accrual statement provides a more complete and accurate picture of the store's financial results.

## Financial Statements: The Balance Sheet

Accounting systems function to generate reports that provide an accurate picture of a business's financial condition and performance. There are two standard financial reports prepared by businesses: the balance sheet and the income statement (also called a profit and loss statement or a statement of revenues and expenses). For the firm's owners and managers, these reports inform decisions about the firm's management, operations, and capital spending. Economic development professionals use this information to make decisions about whether to provide debt or equity financing to a firm. Practitioners also use financial statement analysis in their technical assistance work, to identify weaknesses and management issues that firms need to address to improve their performance and access financing. Although the balance sheet and income statement are separate reports, they are closely linked and should be analyzed together to understand a firm's finances. A third financial report, the cash flow statement, details how the firm's activities affect cash flow. While a cash flow statement is included in audited financial statements prepared by independent accounting firms, firms without audited statements often do not prepare this key financial statement themselves. Thus, the steps to construct a cash flow statement from the balance sheet and income statement are detailed below.

The *balance sheet* is a snapshot of a business's financial position at a single point in time. It organizes financial information about the firm's assets (things of value that it owns), liabilities (its financial obligations), and shareholder's equity on a specific date. Exhibit 3.2 presents the balance sheet for a fictional firm, American Biotechnology Company (ABC). Note that the balance sheet includes a date, June 30, 2002, which is the date for which the report applies. The asset and liability values listed in the report are for that specific date. Since ABC may undertake transactions that significantly change its financial position on the next day, this static picture is an important limitation of the financial information in a balance sheet. As the name implies, the balance sheet must balance; that is, the total assets must equal the total liabilities and shareholders' equities, per the dual aspect principle and the dual entry accounting method. ABC's total assets and total liabilities and shareholders' equity both equal $81.8 million.

There are two common interpretations of the balance sheet.4 The first interpretation is a statement of the firm's resources and the claims against those resources. Assets correspond to the resources owned by the firm while the liabilities and shareholders' equity are the claims against those assets. Liabilities are the claims of suppliers, lenders, and other outside parties while shareholders' equity represents the claims of the firm's owners. Thus, one immediate piece of information that the balance sheet provides is the relative size of the claims of outside creditors versus those of the firm's owners. In ABC's case, owner's claims, at $62.9 million, are over three times those of outsiders, at $18.9 million. A second interpretation of the balance sheet is a statement of the firm's sources and uses of funds. The liabilities and shareholders' equity represent the sources of funds while the assets show how the firm used these funds. This view is very useful since it tells us how the firm has financed itself and what assets it has acquired with this financing.

For ABC, shareholders' equity provided the primary source of funds, and the largest uses of these funds have been for property, plant, and equipment ($21.3 million) and purchased technology and goodwill ($19.3 million). Financial information in the balance sheets is reported under specific categories. While the categories in each firm's balance sheet can vary somewhat, 5 Figure 3.2 includes the major categories listed on most balance sheets. Figures on the balance sheet reflect the original cost paid for items, not their current market value.6 "Book value" is often used to refer to this cost valuation of a firm's assets on its financial statements. Assets are grouped into two types: current assets and noncurrent assets. Current assets are those assets that are normally converted into cash within 1 year or, in some cases, within the normal operating cycle of the business. For example, since large aircraft take longer than 1 year to manufacture, the inventory of an aircraft manufacturer represents the materials that would be converted to cash under their normal production and sales cycle, rather than over 1 year. Assets are listed in a specific order, with those most easily converted into cash (referred to as more "liquid" assets) listed first followed by less liquid assets. Thus, current assets are listed before noncurrent assets, and cash is the first item listed.

The current asset categories on ABC's balance sheet are cash, marketable securities, accounts receivable, inventory, and prepaid expenses. *Cash* refers to both cash that is in the firm's direct possession and funds held in ABC's bank accounts that are immediately available for its use. *Marketable securities* are investment securities with maturities of 1 year or less that can be readily redeemed or sold. Firms often have more cash than they need for near term expenditures, and they invest these funds in certificates of deposit, commercial paper, treasury bills, or other short-term investment instruments to increase interest income earned on these funds. *Accounts receivables* are the uncollected bills for goods and services that ABC has shipped or rendered. Since most businesses do not operate on a cash sales basis, accounts receivable are usually a large and important part of a firm's current assets. ABC's accounts receivables total $16 million, almost one fifth of its total assets. *Inventory* refers to goods held by the firm in one of three forms:

(1) raw materials and supplies that are used in the firm's business;

(2) unfinished goods-in-progress that the firm is still in the process of manufacturing; and

(3) finished products.

Some firms list inventory under these three separate categories on their balance, but others, like ABC, consolidate all three types of inventory into one figure. Inventory is a major asset for some business, such as manufacturers, retailers, and wholesalers, but is of little significance to service businesses. *Prepaid expenses,* the final current asset category, are costs that the business has paid for but that are not yet treated as expenses based on the matching concept. Businesses often pay in advance for expenses recognized in future periods. For example, a firm may pay for an annual insurance policy in advance of the policy period. This advance payment is an asset, something of value that the firm acquired that will be used in the future course of its business. The prepaid expense amount will be reduced each month of the period covered by the policy, as the business "uses" its insurance policy. An accounting entry will be made to record a business expense equal to the reduction in the prepaid expense asset.7

ABC's noncurrent assets, those with a life longer than 1 year, include property, plant, and equipment; purchased technology and goodwill; and other assets. *Property, plant, and equipment* represent the land, buildings, and equipment owned by the business. These items are often listed under the term *fixed assets* since they are, with the exception of noninstalled equipment, immovable. Since property, plant, and equipment have a limited useful life, firms reduce the value of their fixed assets each year to account for the implicit costs associated with their wearing out and replacement over time.

The term for this reduction in value of fixed assets is *depreciation*. Thus, ABC's $21.9 million of property, plant, and equipment is listed net of accumulated depreciation: the figure represents the original cost of these assets less the cumulative depreciation deductions taken. Other firms list the original cost, accumulated depreciation, and the net value as separate items on their balance sheet. When a business depreciates the value of its fixed assets, it enters a corresponding accounting entry as a depreciation expense on the income statement. Purchased technology and goodwill represents the value of other firms and technology acquired by ABC. When a firm acquires the assets of another firm, it may pay more than the stated book value of its assets. Accountants use *goodwill* to account for this excess of the acquisition price over the book value.

Goodwill may relate to acquired assets that have real value to firms, such as brand names, customer lists, experience, and relationships, but that cannot be directly valued. Goodwill also can reflect the difference between a firm's book value and its market value at the time of acquisition. *Other assets* is a catchall category for other things owned by the firm that do not fit into other categories or do not warrant a separate listing. The equities side of the balance sheet is divided into two sections, liabilities and shareholders' equity. As with assets, liabilities to be paid within either 1 year or the business's normal operating cycle are listed first under current liabilities. ABC's balance sheet includes the typical current liabilities categories: accounts payable, income taxes payable, accrued expenses, deferred income, and current portion of long-tem debt. *Accounts payable* are ABC's unpaid bills for goods and services that it received as of June 30, 2002. Accounts payable and accounts receivable are two sides of the same transaction.

One firm's account receivable is another's account payable. An account receivable is the vendor's uncollected invoice for goods or services rendered; an account payable is the customer's unpaid bill for goods or services received. *Income taxes payable* are ABC's unpaid portion of its tax liability on its net income from the prior period. Depending on the applicable state and local taxes, a firm may have additional tax liabilities for property, excise, and other taxes. *Accrued expenses* is a concept similar to prepaid expenses. It refers to expenses that have been recognized for accounting purposes but have not yet been billed or paid. With the matching of revenue and expenses under accrual accounting, costs are recognized as expenses for a period if they are directly tied to goods or services delivered during that period or are general expenses for the period. When such a cost is recognized as expense in a period but has not yet been billed or paid, there is an associated liability for that expense item.

Interest payments are a good example of accrued expenses. Some debt contracts require interest payments every quarter or 6 months, but the firm is incurring an interest payment obligation each month. The interest obligation will be deducted as an expense each month. This interest expense is not paid monthly but builds up, or accrues, as an obligation to be paid at a future date. Accrued expenses can also be viewed as the opposite of prepaid expenses. For prepaid expenses, a firm generates an asset by paying for expenses in advance of their "use." With accrued expenses, a firm creates a liability by "using" an expense before it has been billed or paid. *Deferred income* refers to an obligation to provide goods or service for which ABC received advance payment. For example, ABC may have entered into research and development contracts and received up front payment for some of these activities. If ABC needs to acquire facilities and equipment and hire scientists before it can begin the research, it might be paid for some costs in advance.

Although ABC has received cash, it cannot recognize this payment as revenue, since under the realization concept it has not provided these services yet. Thus the advance payment is offset by a deferred income liability for the same amount. The deferred income liability will be reduced as the company completes the research and development services and recognizes the revenue for these activities. ABC has a second deferred income liability that is not listed under current liabilities. This means that ABC received advance payment for obligations that extend beyond 1 year. The portion of the advance payment for research activities over the next year is listed under current liabilities while the balance is listed as a noncurrent liability. *Current portion of long-term debt,* the last current liability listed on ABC's balance sheet, is the portion of ABC's total outstanding debt that must be repaid over the next year.

As with deferred income, the balance sheet divides debt liabilities into two portions: the amount payable over the next year and the amount payable beyond 1 year. Only the principal component of debt is listed on the balance sheet. Interest payments are an expense included on the income statement. To calculate ABC's total debt service for a given year from its financial statements, one needs to sum the interest expense from the income statement for that year (interest payments) and the current portion of long-term debt from the balance sheet for the end of the prior year (principal payments).

Shareholders' equity completes the equity side of the balance sheet. The presentation of shareholders' equity can be confusing since it includes three parts:

(1) par value;

(2) additional paid-in capital; and

(3) accumulated retained earnings or deficit.

*Par value* is a stated value for the stock that is legally required. It does not have any relationship to the stock's actual market value. Since the par value is the lowest value at which a share of stock can trade, it is usually set at one cent ($.01). Thus, the balance sheet lists the stock's par value as the number of issued shares of stock times the par value.

Common stock issue, par value $.01 per share

Authorized 40,000,000 shares,

Issued 23,305,000 shares 233,305

This line means that ABC is legally authorized to sell up to 40 million shares of common stock, but had issued only 23.305 million of these shares as of June 30, 2002. With a par value of $.01, the total par value of the issued shares is $233,305. However, firms do not sell their stock at par value. Instead, they receive a higher amount of money when their stock is sold to shareholders. This difference between the actual funds raised from stock sales and the listed par value is shown on the balance sheet as *additional paid-in capital.* For ABC, additional paid-in capital is $110,198,695. The total amount that ABC raised from its stock sales is $110,432,000, the sum of par value and additional paid-in capital.

The final component of shareholder equity, *retained earnings,* represents the increase in equity value from the accumulated reinvestment of the company's profits (net income). When a business earns a profit, it can distribute some or all of these profits to its shareholders as dividends. The portion that is not paid out as dividends is reinvested in the company and called retained earnings. Since net income represents the firm's residual income after all expenses, it belongs to the firm's owners and any portion retained by the businesses represents an increase in shareholders' equity. Another way to think about this accounting relationship is that when net income is reinvested in a business, it increases the company's assets. Since no external party provided the funds to increase these assets, there is no increase in liabilities to external parties. Consequently, the owners must have a claim on the increased assets, and the owners' equity account increases to balance the increase in assets.

In ABC's case, the balance sheet shows an accumulated deficit of $47.5 million rather than accumulated retained earnings. This means that the company has generated more losses over its life than profits. Its accumulated losses, after deducting any accumulated net income, total $47.5 million. ABC invested its equity to fund research and development and other activities that have not yet generated sufficient revenues to earn sustained profits. Its up front investment to acquire technology and develop new products has exceeded its cumulative profits.

This is a common situation for biotechnology companies, which have long lead times, often 10 years or longer, before a new product is developed, tested, and approved for use by regulators. These accumulated losses serve to reduce the book value of the shareholder equity in the same manner that retained earnings increase it. Accumulated losses diminish the firm's assets, which must be consumed to cover the excess of expenses over revenues.8 Since assets have declined without any reduction in liabilities, the value of the shareholders' claim has been reduced. ABC's losses reduced the book value of shareholders' equity from $110.4 million to $62.9 million. It is important to recognize that this book value for shareholder equity is not the same as the market value of the firm's stock. ABC's stock price may have increased, despite the accumulated losses, if investors believe that the company has good future earning prospects.

## The Income Statement

The second major financial statement produced by firms is the *income statement,* also referred to as a *profit and loss statement* or a *statement of revenue and expenses.* While the balance sheet presents a firm's financial position at one point in time, the income statement shows the financial results from a business's activities over a period of time. It summarizes the two parts of a company's financial flows that determine its profits: revenues and expenses. By relating a firm's expenses to its revenue over a period of time, the income statement presents the economic results of the firm's activities for that period (i.e., its profits).

Revenue is listed on the top of the income statement with expenses listed below and net income (profit) presented at the bottom. Beyond this general format, firms use many different presentations of revenue and expenses for their income statement.

The main variation occurs in how expenses are separated to present different subtotals before the final net income line. For ABC, income before interest and taxes (known as IBIT or EBIT—for earnings before interest and taxes) is presented as a separate item before the final net income figure is calculated. This allows the reader to see the firm's profits without financing and tax costs. Another common format calculates a gross margin before deducting selling, general, and administrative costs, which helps in understanding the firm's core profitability from operations before administrative, sales, and overhead costs are considered.

ABC lists three sources of income: product sales, research and development, and interest income. *Product sales* and *research and development revenue* account for the revenue realized during the 12 months from each respective activity. Interest income is revenue earned from the company's investment of surplus cash in marketable securities. Since the income statement presents separate expense figures for manufactured products and research and development activities, it is possible to determine a gross profit for each activity.

*Gross profit* (also known as *gross margin*) is the difference between revenue and the direct costs involved in producing goods or delivering services. *Costs of goods sold* is the name used for the direct expenses incurred by ABC to make its products, including materials, labor, energy, and other items. The gross margin for ABC's product sales is calculated by subtracting the costs of goods sold from product sales:

Gross margin for products = 5,013,000 “ 4,967,000 = 46,000

From these figures, it is clear that ABC's R&D activities are more profitable than its manufacturing business, by a factor of over 100! Looking only at ABC's bottom line net income masks this difference. A useful way to present gross margin is as a percentage of sales. ABC's *gross margin percentage* for each activity is Gross margin percentage on product sales = 47,000 = 0.9%

5,013,000

Gross margin percentage on R&D = 5,598,000 = 72.9%

7,675,000

ABC's next expense item is *selling, general, and administrative costs,* or SGA expense. SGA includes all the indirect expense of the firm, including the salaries for executives, salespeople, the accounting department, and other general overhead such as insurance and real estate costs for administrative offices.

The following expense item is depreciation, which we touched upon in the discussion of fixed assets. *Depreciation* is a noncash expense that accounts for the diminution in an asset's value over time. Depreciation is deducted as an expense to represent this economic cost to a business, but it has no impact on ABC's cash flow. ABC never writes a check or makes a payment for its depreciation expense.

After SGA and depreciation expenses, ABC reports its income before interest and taxes. This earnings amount is often referred to as *operating profits* since it measures a firm's earnings from all its operations before the impact of financing, taxes, or other nonoperating expenses are considered. Like gross margin, operating profit is more informative when expressed as a percentage of total revenue. ABC's operating profit percentage was 15.3% of revenue in fiscal year 2002.[9] The final net income figure is listed after deducting interest expenses on ABC's debt and a provision to cover expected tax payments. ABC's net income in FY2002 was $1,754,000, or 13.6% of sales. Thus, interest and taxes had only a small impact of ABC's net income, reducing it by less than 2 percentage points.

The final part of the income statement reports dividend payments to shareholders and retained earnings. In ABC's case, there were no dividend payments in this year. All of its $1,754,000 in net income was retained for reinvestment in the business. In the final lines of the income statement, retained earnings for the current year are added to the retained earnings at the beginning of the year to calculate ABC's final retained earnings as of June 30, 2002. Since ABC has generated cumulative losses during its lifetime, it has "negative retained earnings" which is called an *accumulated deficit.* The $1,754,000 in retained earnings for FY2002, therefore, reduced its accumulated deficit from $49,254,000 to $47,500,000. These last three lines of the income statement formally connect the income statement to the balance sheet. Referring back to ABC's June 30, 2002, balance sheet in Figure 3.1, note that the accumulated deficit under shareholders' equity is $47,500,000, matching the income statement's figure for accumulated deficit at year end.

## Connecting the Balance

Thus far, we have only touched on the interrelationship between the balance sheet and income statement. However, these two financial statements are closely connected, with two ways to view their interaction.

In the first view, two balance sheets and the intervening income statement provide a full picture of a firm's financial performance and change in financial condition for a given period. The beginning and ending balance sheets for a year show the changes in assets, liabilities, and owners' equity whereas the income statement shows how revenue and expense flows contribute to these balance sheet changes over that year. One direct connection is that retained earnings from net income on the income statement increases shareholders' equity on the balance sheet.

Another direct connection occurs when an expense item on the income statement is coupled with a decrease in an asset account (e.g., when a depreciation expense on the income statement is matched with the depreciation of fixed assets). In this manner, decreases in an asset account, such as prepaid expenses, inventory, and fixed assets are often connected to an increase in expenses. On the other hand, sales generate an increase in accounts receivable, an asset account.

The change in accounts receivable from one balance sheet to another is a function of two things: new accounts receivables created by sales and the conversion of accounts receivables into cash through their collection.

Finally, the sale of an asset can result in revenue on the income statement. When the asset is sold for more than its book value, it yields income called capital gains. Conversely, when the firm sells an asset for less than its book value, it has a capital loss. By relating income statement items to the balance sheet, we gain a deeper understanding of what accounts for balance sheet changes.

A second way to view the interrelationship of the balance sheet and income statement is through the lens of cash flow (i.e., how both contribute to a firm's cash flow). The income statement generates cash flow through the excess of revenue over expenses. To the extent that revenue and expenses are fully converted into cash transactions, net income is a good proxy for cash flow.

However, since financial statements are not based on cash transactions, they need to be adjusted to present their contribution to cash flow. One type of adjustment corrects for noncash expenses such as depreciation. A second type of adjustment captures the impact of balance sheet changes on cash flow. For example, the cash flow from sales is affected by the collection of accounts receivable.

When accounts receivable increase over a year, this reduces the cash flow realized from sales. Net income must be reduced by this increase in accounts receivable to show actual cash flow for the period. An increase in other asset accounts, such as inventory or fixed assets, results from the firm converting cash into other assets.

Thus, the general rule is that increases in asset accounts are a use of cash (i.e., decrease cash flow). Increases in liability accounts are a source of cash that increase cash flow. A clear example of this is when a firm secures new debt; it receives cash from the debt proceeds as the liability for outstanding debt increases. When accounts payable increase, this represents an increase in the firm's unpaid bills, which means that some of the expenses shown on the income statement were not converted into cash outlays. Thus, an addition to net income is made equal to the increase in accounts payable to show actual cash flow. These examples demonstrate that both the income statement and balance sheet must be analyzed to determine a firm's cash flow over a period.

### The Cash Flow Statement

As indicated above, *the cash flow statement* details how a firm's income statement and changes to its balance sheet accounts contribute to cash flow for a specific period. It may seem surprising that cash flow statements are prepared since earlier in this chapter it was argued that accrual financial statements provide a more accurate picture of a firm's economic performance than cash basis statements. If accrual statements are more accurate, why bother with cash flow analysis? The answer is twofold. First, a company needs cash flow to pay its bills and make debt service payments.

Although accrual statements provide a better picture of a business's economic profits than a cash flow statement, a firm does not pay its bills with profits. We need to know the firm's actual cash flow to determine whether it can meet the payments for a proposed loan. Second, cash flow statements provide insight into how a firm generates and uses cash flow, which can indicate areas for improved management and operations. For example, if a profitable company experiences cash flow problems due to large increases in its accounts receivables, then it needs to change its credit policies and collection practices.

Another argument against preparing a cash flow statement is that a business's net cash flow for a period is revealed by the change in the balance sheet cash account for that period. By definition, the change in cash from one period to another is the firm's net cash flow. Why undertake the tedious work of constructing a cash flow statement when net cash flow is already known? Although net cash flow is significant, it is more important to understand what contributed to this end result. A firm that loses money from its core business, but has positive cash flow from the onetime sale of assets, is quite different from one with positive cash flow from its core operations and after other costs. Moreover, we do not know how the firm's cash flow related to its level of debt payments. A firm with $40,000 in net cash flow and $30,000 in annual debt service is a better credit risk than a business with the same net cash flow but debt payments of $250,000.

## CONSTRUCTING A CASH FLOW STATEMENT

A statement of cash flows is included in the standard audited financial statements prepared by a firm's independent accountants. Since many privately held companies, and most small businesses, do not produce audited financial statements, practitioners need to know how to prepare a cash flow statement for a specific period. To prepare a cash flow statement, the balance sheets for the beginning and end of the period and the income statement for the period are necessary. Two types of adjustments are made to the income statement to determine cash flow:

(1) noncash expense items (e.g., depreciation) are added back; and

(2) cash flows from changes in balance sheet accounts are incorporated.

When preparing a cash flow statement, it is helpful to divide the statement into three sets of activities that affect cash flow: operations (purchasing, production, and sales activities); investment activities (purchase of plant and equipment to support operations); and financing activities (securing or retiring debt and equity). Beyond showing the relative impact of operations, investment, and financing on a firm's cash flow, this format simplifies the calculation of debt service coverage ratios. It highlights the cash flow available to make debt service payments (i.e., the cash flow prior to financing activities) and the principal and interest payments for the period. For these reasons, the following explanation and example organizes the cash flow statement into these three components: cash flow from operations, cash flow from investments, and cash flow from financing. This is not the only way to present a cash flow statement, but it is well suited to analyzing a business's borrowing capacity.

The first step in cash flow analysis is finding the correct starting point from the firm's income statement. Since we need to compare cash flow to debt payments, the starting figure should exclude the interest expense. Therefore, begin with *net income before interest and tax payments,* which many firms list as a separate line on the income statement as income (or earnings) before interest and taxes (IBIT). Next, subtract the tax payments (or allowance for taxes) from the IBIT amount. When IBIT is not listed as a separate line on the income statement, begin with the final figure for net income after interest and taxes and add back the interest payment amount. Once net income after taxes and before interest payments is determined, the second step is adding back noncash expense items, which are accounting items that were subtracted from revenues as an economic expense but do not involve a real cash outflow. Depreciation is the most common noncash item, but amortization of patents, goodwill, and other costs is a second example.

Third, incorporate the cash flow impact from balance sheet changes related to operating activities, for both assets and liabilities/owners' equity. The relevant asset accounts are accounts receivable, inventory, prepaid expenses, and other noninvestment related accounts. Liability accounts for this portion of the cash flow analysis are accounts payable, accrued expenses, deferred income, other payable accounts, and other liability accounts that are not debt or equity financing items. An increase in an asset account is a cash outflow (use of cash) that is a negative entry on the cash flow statement. Conversely, a decrease in an asset account is a cash inflow (source of cash) treated as a positive entry on the cash flow statement. Consider accounts receivable to see the relationship between asset accounts and cash flow. An increase in accounts receivable means that uncollected sales are higher, which reduces the cash flow received from the sales revenue shown on the income statement. If accounts receivable decrease, cash collections from sales exceed the sales revenue on the income statement, generating a cash flow increase. Liability accounts have the opposite effect on cash flow: a decrease in a liability account is a cash outflow, whereas a liability account increase is a cash inflow. For example, when deferred income increases, the firm has received additional cash that is not included in the period's revenue on the income statement but needs to be added to represent true cash flow.

If deferred income decreases, the business recognized some deferred income as revenue on its income statement in the period, although the associated cash inflow occurred in a prior period. Thus, a cash outflow deduction from net income is made to reflect the cash effect of the deferred income change. Once the cash flow impact of these balance sheet accounts is determined, they are summed up and added to the earlier figure for net income before interest payment plus noncash expenses.

The resulting sum is *net cash flow from operations*. It indicates whether the firm is generating positive or negative cash flow from its core purchasing, production, and sales activities. A negative cash flow may indicate management problems, such as carrying too much inventory or slow accounts receivable collection. However, it may also indicate a well-managed firm that is expanding its inventory and accounts receivables as its sales grow, using internal cash flow to finance them.

In the second part of the cash flow analysis, the cash impact from investment activities is calculated. Investment activities include the purchase of long-term assets to support the firm's operations and expand sales. These investments are shown on the balance sheet as increases in fixed asset accounts (plant and equipment), patents or purchased technology, and goodwill (intangible assets from the purchase of other businesses). A second type of investment activity is using excess cash to acquire marketable securities or other financial investments. Changes in any of these asset accounts are included in the investment activity part of the cash flow analysis. As with the operating assets, increases in these accounts are a cash outflow while decreases represent a cash inflow.

In this case, it is intuitive that when a business purchases new equipment, for example, it uses cash; and when a fixed asset account declines, the firm is selling the asset and generating cash. *These* changes must be calculated based on the gross value asset accounts before *any depreciation or amortization.* The change in gross value represents the actual cash transaction without the confusion of noncash deductions. Calculate the cash flow impact from changes in each investment-related account and then add these figures to the net cash flow from operations. The resulting figure is *net cash flow after investing activities.* This figure is used to determine the debt service coverage ratio, since it represents the firm's cash flow prior to its debt service payments and other financing activities.

The final step incorporates the impact of the firm's financing transactions (i.e., new borrowing and stock sales, the repayment of debt, interest payments, and dividend payments) on cash flow. For this analysis, include both balance sheet and income statement items. From the balance sheet, calculate changes in debt accounts and total proceeds from stock sales. Since debt is divided into two accounts, current portion of long-term debt and long-term debt, the change in the sum of these two accounts must be calculated to determine the change in total debt. When this sum increases, there is a cash inflow from additional borrowing. On the other hand, when the sum of the current and long-term portions of debt declines, it represents a cash outflow from the firm to pay-down of debt.

Debt-related cash flow also includes interest payments, which are obtained from the interest expense item on the income statement. For equity financing, cash flow from stock issuance equals the change in the total shareholders' paid-in capital. Total paid-in capital is the sum of stock par value and additional paid-in capital from the shareholders' equity section of the balance sheet. Note that retained earnings are excluded since they were already counted within the firm's net income.

If the change in retained earnings is added, it will double count this portion of net income. An increase in total paid-in equity capital represents cash inflow from additional stock sales. A decrease indicates the use of cash to buy back stock. The final item included in cash flow from financing activities is the deduction of dividend payments itemized on the income statement. For the final net cash flow calculation, sum the cash flow changes from all the financing accounts and add them to net cash from after investing activity. This final figure, cash flow after financing activities, is the firm's *net cash flow*. To check the accuracy of the cash flow analysis, compare this net cash flow figure to the change in the balance sheet cash account for the period. The two figures should be identical.

## Using Financial Statements

This chapter provided an introduction to the language, presentation, and organization of business financial statements. With this knowledge, the reader is prepared to develop skills in analyzing business financial statements to inform economic development finance decisions. Although information in financial statements can be used for a variety of purposes, the primary goal of economic development practitioners is to evaluate the firm's financial health, its capacity to productively use new debt or equity, and the appropriate structure for any new financing. The next chapter provides a framework and financial tools to undertake this type of analysis.

This Strategic Framework is one of a number of Operational Strategy documents produced to guide the delivery of activity in support of the 2007-2013 Convergence and Competitiveness ERDF and ESF Programmes in Wales. There are spatially-driven Frameworks covering the six areas identified in the Wales Spatial Plan and thematically-driven Frameworks. All the Frameworks can be viewed on the WEFO Website. They have two specific purposes:

- To guide prospective project sponsors as to the strategic approach that partners in Wales have agreed should be taken to delivering on the aims, objectives and targets set out in the Convergence and Competitiveness ERDF and ESF Operational Programmes and to help them identify the extent to which their project idea can contribute to programme delivery.
- To assist WEFO in selecting and prioritising projects (fit with a Strategic Framework being one of the selection and prioritisation criteria) and in the overall management, monitoring and evaluation of a balanced programme.

Over the life of the programme, as conditions change, the operational strategies set out in the Framework documents may need to change also; therefore each framework will be subject to on-going monitoring, evaluation and review. The arrangements for the ongoing maintenance of this framework are set out in section 9 below.

This Framework covers the *second theme*, Business Finance, in *Priority 2* of the *Convergence ERDF* Operational Programme and *Priority 2* of the *Competitiveness ERDF* Operational Programme (OPs).

Before approaching WEFO about a project idea, prospective sponsors should first of all assure themselves of its fit with the framework and should examine the WEFO website to see which other project ideas are being worked up in the same field. Any possibility of partnership collaboration with other organisations should be explored at an early stage, collaboration being another of the criteria by which WEFO will select and prioritise projects.

## Partnerships involved in developing and maintaining this Framework

The Business Finance Framework is of potential interest to a wide range of partners and stakeholders. In addition to responding to enquiries received via the WEFO website, the Framework Coordinator's engagement with partners/ stakeholders is as follows:

### *Welsh Local Government Association (WLGA)*

The WLGA held a consultation event on 28 July 2007. A representative from DE&T attended the event. Written feedback was collated following the event however no comment was made on this Framework.

### *Federation of Small Businesses (FSB)*

A copy of the Framework has been forwarded to the Chief Executive of the FSB requesting its dissemination to members for comment and feedback. There has been no comment to date.

### *Confederation of British Industry (CBI)*

A copy of the Framework has been forwarded to the Chief Executive of the CBI requesting its dissemination to members for comment and feedback. There has been no comment to date.

### *Welsh Council for Voluntary Action (WCVA)*

The WCVA held a consultation event on 1 June 2007 which included representatives from the third sector. The Framework was presented to members and a question and answer session was held. The feedback channels available to members were outlined.

### *All Wales Ethnic Minority Association (AWEMA)*

A copy of the Framework has been forwarded to the Chief Executive of the AWEMA requesting its dissemination to members for comment and feedback. There has been no comment to date.

### *Chwarae Teg*

A copy of the Framework has been forwarded to the Chief Executive asking for comment and feedback. A response was received from Chwarae Teg and their comments have been considered.

### *Social Enterprise Network*

Representatives of the Social Enterprise Network were present at the WCVA-led third sector consultation event in June.

### *Wales Social Partners*

The Framework will be presented to the Partners at the Business Wales event on 3 September 2007.

Future engagement on this Framework will not be confined exclusively to these organisations.

The Framework is also seeking engagement with the partnerships supporting development of other relevant Frameworks.

## Links with Other Frameworks and EU Initiatives

It is important for projects to find the right programme, priority, theme and framework to cover their proposed activity. It is not always immediately obvious which of these is most appropriate; this section is intended to give guidance to prospective project sponsors. It also sets out issues of coherent planning that extend across programme / framework boundaries. Reference should be made to the documents named in this section in order to ensure strategic coherence and synergy with other plans.

Activities supported under this Framework have the potential to compliment a range of initiatives falling under other frameworks and it is not possible to be prescriptive over the list of frameworks that you should consider when proposing actions under this Framework. However, at the very least you should look at those frameworks involving possible support to enterprises which include R&D and Innovation, Enterprise, Materials Efficiency and Community Economic Development.

The principles set out in this Framework, and in particular in Section 8 below, will be applied to any proposals for financial interventions to individuals, businesses or other organisations developed as part of projects relating to other Frameworks in the Convergence and Competitiveness Programmes.

The Framework also links to the European Commission's JEREMIE (Joint European Resources for Micro to Medium Enterprises) initiative which will enable European Member States and Regions to use part of their Structural Funds to obtain a set of financial instruments that are specifically designed to support micro and small & medium enterprises. Further information will follow on how this might be adopted in Wales. The Framework also links to the Welsh Assembly Government New Operating Model developed for the New Single Investment Fund, which will merge 7 existing Welsh Assembly Government run grant schemes, under one flexible operating model, ensuring a uniform approach is taken in the delivery of Welsh Assembly Government administered financial support.

## The Priority and Themes addressed by this Framework

### *Priority 2: Improving Business Competitiveness*

The aim of this Priority is to strengthen the economy by increasing the size and widening the range of business stock and tackling market failure in relation to business advice, information and finance. (This is consistent with the Lisbon Strategy on 'working together for growth and jobs' and specifically addresses the first strand of improving knowledge and innovation for growth.) Draft – 30 August 2007 4

### *Theme 2: Business Finance*

This Theme aims to assist the growth and expansion of business by improving access to business finance. This will be achieved by:

- Providing debt finance and venture capital to address market failures in financial support mechanisms required to create new SMEs and develop existing ones;
- Providing discretionary focused grant support packages for businesses including, but not limited to, high growth sectors; and
- Supporting and accelerating Welsh exports.

### *Priority 2 Key Indicators, with Particular Relevance to the Framework*

The following are the indicators for Priority 2 (Convergence). Those of particular relevance to this Strategic Framework are highlighted with an asterisk.

Information on targets can be found in the Operational Programme. Guidance and definitions of indicators has been produced by the WEFO Research, Monitoring and Evaluation branch and will be available from the WEFO website www.wefo.wales.gov.uk.

### *Outputs*

Enterprises assisted

Enterprises financially supported*

Social enterprises assisted

Social enterprises financially supported*

Individuals assisted to set up a new enterprise

Individuals financially supported to set up a new enterprise*

### *Results*

Gross jobs created*

Enterprises created

Profit benefit*

Enterprises adopting or improving equality strategies and monitoring systems*

Enterprises adopting or improving Environmental Management Systems*

Investment induced*

Increase in level of export*

### *Impacts*

Net jobs created*

Net enterprises created

Increase in turnover*

Net increase in level of export*

Increase in company-level GVA*

Impact indicators can only be assessed through evaluation - please see Section 9 for more information. Draft – 30 August 2007 5

This Priority aims to strengthen the environment for enterprise by supporting new and existing business ventures, particularly enterprises with the capacity and potential to grow. This will be achieved by:

- supporting the start-up of new enterprises;
- supporting the growth of existing enterprises, particularly those with the capacity to grow;
- promoting opportunities to grow the sectors in which East Wales is strong, or those seeking to develop;
- building the sustainability of community and social enterprises by increasing their contribution; and
- providing targeted debt finance and venture capital to address market failures in financial support mechanisms required to create new SMEs and develop existing ones.

### Priority 2 Key Indicators, with Particular Relevance to the Framework

The following are the indicators for Priority 2 (Competitiveness). Those of particular relevance to this Strategic Framework are highlighted with an asterisk. Information on targets can be found in the Operational Programme.

***Outputs***

Enterprises assisted

Enterprises financially supported*

Social enterprises assisted

Social enterprises financially supported*

Individuals assisted to set up a new enterprise

Individuals financially supported to set up a new enterprise*

***Results***

Gross jobs created*

Enterprises created

Profit benefit*

Enterprises adopting or improving equality strategies and monitoring systems*

Enterprises adopting or improving Environmental Management Systems*

Investment induced*

Increase in level of export*

***Impacts***

Net jobs created*

Net enterprises created

Increase in turnover*

Net increase in level of export*

Increase in company-level GVA*

Impact indicators can only be assessed through evaluation - please see Section 9 for more information.

The Welsh Assembly Government and National Policies & Strategies that are aligned with this Priority and Theme are:

The Wider Strategic Context

- One Wales – A Progressive Agenda for the Government of Wales

- Wales: A Vibrant Economy

Strategies and Policies specific to this Theme

- The Entrepreneurship Action Plan

- Knowledge Bank for Business

- International Trade Strategy for Wales

- Social Enterprise Strategy for Wales

**The Fields of Intervention & Delivery Approaches**

The aim of this Framework is to assist the growth and expansion of business by complementing market provision of finance for new and growing businesses, to raise overall output and create and sustain more value added jobs.

The Framework will do this by improving the efficiency and functioning of Wales' financial markets through targeted intervention alongside the private sector to overcome the market failures in accessing finance.

Under this Framework no single sector will be prioritised to the exclusion of any other although the 10 sectors identified as important to economic growth in Wales: A Vibrant Economy are relevant.

Projects targeted at supporting high growth businesses wishing to invest to improve their global competitiveness, through the development of new products and services or of new export markets, will be of particular interest.

However, it is recognised that certain types of new and established businesses - e.g. social enterprises, enterprises run by women and underrepresented groups, or enterprises located in deprived areas - face particular difficulties in accessing and obtaining finance for their enterprise. This framework will also support projects aimed at overcoming these barriers.

## FINANCIAL SUPPORT INITIATIVES

These could include initiatives such as debt, mezzanine debt & equity/risk capital, seed capital, Business Angel co-investment and micro finance initiatives. These should aim to stimulate demand for and increase the capacity to obtain private sector sources of commercial finance or the provision of public/private debt and venture capital instruments on commercial terms.

### Grant Instruments

The Competitiveness Programme will not support proposals for grant instruments.

For the Convergence Programme, project sponsors/developers should bear in mind the Welsh Assembly Government's policy shift from a grant culture to an investment culture. It is anticipated that this policy shift will be a major consideration in the selection and prioritisation of projects by WEFO. It is therefore expected that proposals for grant instruments will state clearly how they contribute to this policy shift, reduce grant dependency over time and encourage a change in attitude amongst beneficiaries to commercial sources of finance.

In addition, proposals which demonstrate simplification and flexibility from the customer's perspective will be prioritised, e.g. innovation through syndication of grant regimes across geographical or organisational boundaries or through simplification of application/appraisal processes. Proposals could include those designed to stimulate demand for and capacity to obtain private sector sources of commercial finance or the provision of public/private debt and venture capital instruments on commercial terms.

## Trans-National Cooperation

A number of existing networks in the UK and Europe provide opportunities to share and disseminate best practice. Opportunities will also arise to understand and learn from the experiences of other regions in the implementation of the programme.

## The Spatial Context

Projects developed under this Framework will be delivered nationally, regionally and locally. Spatial Plan Groups will advise on the types of projects which best address gaps in provision and tackle local economic development priorities. This applies to both the Convergence and Competitiveness Programmes.

North West Wales Area: Challenges in this area relevant to the Framework: Economic inactivity impacts on the sustainability and diversity of local economies within the area.

Specific spatial areas to be targeted: The areas of North Wales linked to the Sustainable Regeneration Framework including Rhyl, Colwyn Bay, Caernarfon and Holyhead.

Specific beneficiary groups to be targeted: Social Enterprises have the potential to strengthen the local economy through helping to overcome economic inactivity and will continue to diversify the local economy.

Specific areas of opportunities to be exploited by interventions in the Framework: Assistance for Businesses wishing to explore the potential of new export markets;

Assistance for Businesses in high growth areas to improve their competitiveness in global markets through new product development and services; A package of generic support to aid in the start up of new enterprises and develop existing ones; Targeted support for enterprises to grow and develop in the deprived areas within the Sustainable Regeneration Framework for North Wales.

Draft – 30 August 2007 8

Central Wales Area:

Challenges in this area relevant to the Framework:

- The area is predominantly rural and population settlements are dispersed;
- A cost to value gap of buildings exists;
- Flexibility and simplicity in accessing Business Finance.

Specific spatial areas to be targeted:

- The areas of Central Wales linked to the Sustainable Regeneration Framework.

Specific beneficiary groups to be targeted:

- Social Enterprises;
- High Growth and high valued sectors;
- New and existing enterprises.

Specific areas of opportunities to be exploited by interventions in the Framework:

- Financial interventions to bridge the cost to value gap in provision of commercial space for new and developing enterprise;
- Provide enhanced financial support initiatives to non 'commercially attractive' enterprises to encourage and enable access to commercial sources of finance;

- Simplified and flexible financial instruments to support start up of new enterprises and the further development of existing ones;
- Financial support initiatives and instruments which target enterprise in deprived areas linked to the Sustainable Regeneration Framework and other Central Wales regeneration initiatives;
- Support to high growth and high value sectors to improve competitiveness, access to markets and growth through for example second and third stage investment and 'Technium 2' opportunities.

**South East Wales Area**

Challenges in this area relevant to the Framework:

- Flexibility and simplicity in access to Business Finance.

Specific spatial areas to be targeted:

- Targeted spatial support in the Heads of the Valleys.

Specific beneficiary groups to be targeted:

- Sectoral prioritisation of business finance will be towards construction, tourism, creative/cultural industries, manufacturing and environmental technologies businesses.

Specific areas of opportunities to be exploited by interventions in the Framework:

- Whole region integrated grant support packages across boundaries;
- Business finance to assist the growth of businesses within the target industries.

***Pembroke Area***

Specific beneficiary groups to be targeted:

- Focus on supporting key sectors including the knowledge economy, tourism & leisure and environmental goods & services;
- Support the development of the social economy, including credit unions.

Draft – 30 August 2007 9

Specific areas of opportunities to be exploited by interventions in the Framework:

- Provide financial assistance in the form of grants, equity and loans to encourage an equitable spread of prosperity throughout the region to assist businesses to become 'investor ready';
- Provide easy access to financial assistance measures for micro-enterprises and SMEs in sectors important to the region's economy that will achieve higher value economic activity and improved business productivity, efficiency, profitability and sustainability and ultimately a more diverse economy. Assistance will primarily be in capital expenditure and will focus on increasing levels of innovation and R&D as well as supporting greater utilisation of ICT and wherever necessary linked to training support funded through the ESF flexibility;
- Provide revenue support for innovative and more effective marketing, necessary to offset the disadvantages of relative remoteness from key UK and mainland European markets;
- Facilitate private sector investment in industrial and commercial property, including supporting Townscape Heritage Initiative projects;
- Support local authority economic development strategies.

### *Swansea Bay Area*

Challenges in this area relevant to the Framework

- To continue to evolve to a higher value manufacturing and service employment base in a modern competitive economy.

Specific beneficiary groups to be targeted

- Financial Support will build on best practice developed to target SMEs and new enterprises;
- Focus on key sectors including knowledge economy, environmental, energy efficiency, waste management, tourism & leisure, food and bioscience.

Specific Areas of opportunities to be exploited by interventions in the Framework

- Provide financial assistance in the form of grants, equity and loans to encourage an equitable spread of prosperity throughout the region to assist businesses to become 'investor ready';
- Easy access to financial assistance measures for start up and young enterprises including training support funded through 10% ESF flexibility;
- Assist in the integration of business finance with other business support services;
- Support Local Authority economic development strategies;
- Support a change in perception of credit unions so they can develop infrastructure and improve their image to a far greater level than currently exists;
- Emphasis on encouraging enterprise;
- Continued collaborative working based on the strong experience in Swansea Bay.

## The Financial Context

This framework covers Theme 2 under Priority 2 of the Convergence ERDF Programme and Priority 2 of the Regional Employment and Competitiveness ERDF Programme. Financial allocations are fixed at Priority level. Indicative percentages are shown by Theme level; however these are not intended to be absolute allocations for any framework and may shift as the needs of the Programme change.

| Convergence Priority and Theme | Indicative Percentage | Available Funds in the Priority across Convergence Area |
|---|---|---|
| Priority 2 Theme 2 | 53%<br>Note: the intervention rate for the Priority is 47.59% | €192,778,000 (covering both themes within the Priority) |

| Competitiveness Priority | Indicative Percentage | Available Funds in the Priority across Competitiveness Area |
|---|---|---|
| Priority 2 | 40% | € 14,076,400 |

Project sponsors will be expected to obtain match funding either from their own resources or from the private sector; match funding in kind is not appropriate. It is expected that the majority of projects under this framework will have a significant level of Private Sector match funding.

A 10% ESF/ERDF flexibility can be used, where appropriate, to help deliver projects under the Business Finance Framework. The nature of the financial support to be delivered under this Framework will limit the scope to which this flexibility can be applied.

## Key Principles & Regulations affecting Framework Activity

The following principles will apply to activity supported under this Framework and activities under other Frameworks which include financial instruments:-

- Demonstrate strategic fit with the policy shift away from a grant culture towards an investment culture.
- Rigorous understanding and evidence of need.
- No duplication of existing activities. Actions will acknowledge and build on existing activities including those funded under previous European programmes.
- Adhere to 'market failure' principles -- for all proposals, robust and contemporary evidence must be made available that demonstrates market failure either in terms of supply or demand.
- Apply genuine Return on Investment discipline – for all delivery proposals, it will be required that a systematic approach is adopted to understanding the return from the investment to be made.
- Best principles of equality and diversity – for all proposals, clear evidence of how the best principles of equality and diversity will be applied must be presented. This will include both from an organisational and customer perspective, and will also require the maintenance of data and information on an ongoing basis of equality and diversity statistics.
- A priority for the 2007-2013 Programmes and this Strategic Framework is to support major strategic projects rather than a large number of smaller individual projects.
- A priority of this period of Structural Funds in Wales is to achieve greater alignment of supported projects with Welsh Assembly Government policies.
- Activities must demonstrate that they will deliver value for money.
- Projects designed to enable compliance with national or EU legislation will not be supported.

- Project sponsors will be expected to follow the terms of the Welsh Language Board's document on 'Awarding Grants, Loans and Sponsorship' which can be found at www.welsh-language-board.org.uk. The costs of complying with Welsh Language requirements will need to be included in the financial projections for the project. Any translation work (English-Welsh or Welsh-English) required will be paid at a maximum of the Client's rates.
- All projects supported by the framework will need to address the cross cutting themes of Equal Opportunities and Environmental Sustainability. It is important that this occurs at an early stage of project development so that opportunities to support the themes are properly integrated. Guidance for sponsors on the cross cutting themes is available on the WEFO website. Specialist support is also available from the WEFO Cross Cutting Unit.
- Projects supported through the framework will be expected to demonstrate how they will improve on the environmental performance of their business including the development of environmental management systems (EMS) which will assist achievement of the EMS target set for the Priority.

All activity under this Framework will be assessed for compliance with European Commission (EC) State aid rules. WEFO will require assurance that any State aid to be awarded has the necessary EC approval before the aid can be granted.

Aid measures will have the necessary approval if they comply with all the conditions of:

- An existing approved scheme;
- A block exemption regulation; or

- De minimis.

Aid not covered by any of the above will need to be directly notified to the Commission for approval before aid is awarded.

## Framework Evaluation and Progress Review Arrangements

WEFO has responsibility for Programme-level evaluations relating to Structural Fund Programmes, including evaluation of the Strategic Frameworks, and for providing advice to projects on monitoring and evaluation. Further guidance on monitoring and evaluation, including explanations of terminology, has been produced by the WEFO Research, Monitoring and Evaluation (RME) Branch.

### *Strategic Framework evaluation*

WEFO will design, finance, and manage evaluations covering the Strategic Frameworks. Framework Co-ordinators will participate in relevant Evaluation Steering Groups and identify

other relevant evaluation activity being undertaken by WAG or its partners to minimise duplication of activity. Evaluation will take place in the middle and towards the end of the programming period. It will be based on project monitoring data, project-level evaluations and additional fieldwork.

The first stage of evaluation will cover process issues. It will:

- comment on whether and to what extent the Framework is still relevant to the socio-economic circumstances of the area;
- analyse progress to date against key output, result and financial indicators;

- assess whether the Framework is working well as a mechanism for implementing the Programme, including the Cross Cutting Themes;
- investigate how the Framework is interacting with other Frameworks; and
- make practicable recommendations to address any issues found.

The second stage of evaluation will be impact assessment. The key objectives will be:

- assess whether previous evaluation recommendations relevant to the Framework were implemented;
- analyse progress to date against key output, result and financial indicators in the field covered by the Framework; and
- assess current impact, and likely end-Programme impact.

***Project Evaluation***

All projects within the Framework will be required to carry out some form of evaluation, based on project monitoring data and additional fieldwork (for example interviews and surveys) as appropriate. Evaluation plans will be agreed with WEFO at the project development stage. Risky projects (for example, new types of intervention), pilot projects (which are intended to be rolled out more widely), and large projects (those in receipt of over £2 million grant) will be required to commission independent external evaluations to be carried out by specialist research contractors.

All other projects will be required to carry out an evaluation of their own activity. Monitoring and evaluation guidance will be provided to projects by WEFO. Costs associated with evaluation are an eligible project cost.

Project-level evaluations will address the following evaluation questions, as appropriate to the individual project:

- How many net jobs have been created? What has been the quality of any jobs created?
- Has there been any change in turnover of supported enterprises? Is so, to what extent?
- Has there been any change in the net level of export of supported enterprises? If so, to what extent?
- How many net enterprises have been created?
- Has there been any change in company-level GVA of supported enterprises? If so, to what extent?

The evaluation questions must have a clear and logical link with the project's key objectives, and should address the full range of project objectives. To do this, projects should choose questions additional to those listed above in order to ensure that the full scope of project activity is evaluated.

For example, it may be appropriate for some projects creating jobs to look at the demography of people occupying those jobs. WEFO will provide projects with guidance on how to select appropriate questions, and will provide a set of potential questions which projects may wish to use. General guidance on monitoring and evaluation will be available from the RME section of the WEFO website, www.wefo.wales.gov.uk. On-going Framework Review

All Frameworks will be subject to review at any point in the life of the Programmes. The timing of these reviews will be determined by a number of considerations and will be agreed between WEFO, the Framework Co-ordinators and the relevant partners, including the PMC.

One obvious trigger for review will be the results of evaluations undertaken and, as a minimum all Frameworks will therefore be reviewed at an appropriate point around the middle of the programming period.

## Framework Communication and Dissemination

The partnerships listed in section 2 above have an ongoing role in the development and maintenance of this Framework; however the Framework co-ordinator is also keen to ensure that there is the widest possible engagement. Interested stakeholders may find that their organisations have a route to involvement through membership of one of the named partnerships; but they also have the opportunity to comment on the Framework via the website. The Framework Co-ordinator will be monitoring the comments that are posted and they and their partnerships will take account of them in developing the Framework.

9

# RAISING FINANCE

When a company is growing rapidly, for example when contemplating investment in capital equipment or an acquisition, its current financial resources may be inadequate.

Few growing companies are able to finance their expansion plans from cash flow alone. They will therefore need to consider raising finance from other external sources. In addition, managers who are looking to buy-in to a business ("management buy-in" or "MBI") or buy-out (management buy-out" or "MBO") a business from its owners, may not have the resources to acquire the company.

They will need to raise finance to achieve their objectives. There are a number of potential sources of finance to meet the needs of a growing business or to finance an MBI or MBO:

- Existing shareholders and directors funds
- Family and friends
- Business angels
- Clearing banks (overdrafts, short or medium term loans)
- Factoring and invoice discounting
- Hire purchase and leasing

- Merchant banks (medium to longer term loans)
- Venture capital

A key consideration in choosing the source of new business finance is to strike a balance between equity and debt to ensure the funding structure suits the business. The main differences between borrowed money (debt) and equity are that bankers request interest payments and capital repayments, and the borrowed money is usually secured on business assets or the personal assets of shareholders and/or directors. A bank also has the power to place a business into administration or bankruptcy if it defaults on debt interest or repayments or its prospects decline.

In contrast, equity investors take the risk of failure like other shareholders, whilst they will benefit through participation in increasing levels of profits and on the eventual sale of their stake. However in most circumstances venture capitalists will also require more complex investments (such as preference shares or loan stock) in additional to their equity stake. The overall objective in raising finance for a company is to avoid exposing the business to excessive high borrowings, but without unnecessarily diluting the share capital. This will ensure that the financial risk of the company is kept at an optimal level.

## Business Plan

Once a need to raise finance has been identified it is then necessary to prepare a business plan. If management intend to turn around a business or start a new phase of growth, a business plan is an important tool to articulate their ideas while convincing investors and other people to support it. The business plan should be updated regularly to assist in forward planning. There are many potential contents of a business plan. The European Venture Capital Association suggest the following:

- Profiles of company founders directors and other key managers;
- Statistics relating to sales and markets;
- Names of potential customers and anticipated demand;
- Names of, information about and assessment of competitors;
- Financial information required to support specific projects (for example, major capital investment or new product development);
- Research and development information;
- Production process and sources of supply;
- Information on requirements for factory and plant;
- Magazine and newspaper articles about the business and industry;
- Regulations and laws that could affect the business product and process protection (patents, copyrights, trademarks).

The challenge for management in preparing a business plan is to communicate their ideas clearly and succinctly. The very process of researching and writing the business plan should help clarify ideas and identify gaps in management information about their business, competitors and the market.

## TYPES OF FINANCE

A brief description of the key features of the main sources of business finance is provided below.

### Venture Capital

Venture capital is a general term to describe a range of ordinary and preference shares where the investing institution acquires a share in the business. Venture capital is intended for higher risks such as start up situations and development capital for more mature investments. Replacement capital brings in an institution in place of one of the original shareholders of a business who wishes to realise their personal equity before the other shareholders. There are over 100 different venture capital funds in the UK and some have geographical or industry preferences. There are also certain large industrial companies which have funds available to invest in growing businesses and this 'corporate venturing' is an additional source of equity finance.

## Grants and Soft Loans

Government, local authorities, local development agencies and the European Union are the major sources of grants and soft loans. Grants are normally made to facilitate the purchase of assets and either the generation of jobs or the training of employees. Soft loans are normally subsidised by a third party so that the terms of interest and security levels are less than the market rate. There are over 350 initiatives from the Department of Trade and Industry alone so it is a matter of identifying which sources will be appropriate in each case.

## Invoice Discounting and Invoice Factoring

Finance can be raised against debts due from customers via invoice discounting or invoice factoring, thus improving cash flow. Debtors are used as the prime security for the lender and the borrower may obtain up to about 80 per cent of approved debts. In addition, a number of these sources of finance will now lend against stock and other assets and may be more suitable then bank lending. Invoice discounting is normally confidential (the customer is not aware that their payments are essentially insured) whereas factoring extends the simple discounting principle by also dealing with the administration of the sales ledger and debtor collection.

### Hire Purchase and Leasing

Hire purchase agreements and leasing provide finance for the acquisition of specific assets such as cars, equipment and machinery involving a deposit and repayments over, typically, three to ten years. Technically, ownership of the asset remains with the lessor whereas title to the goods is eventually transferred to the hirer in a hire purchase agreement.

### Loans

Medium term loans (up to seven years) and long term loans (including commercial mortgages) are provided for specific purposes such as acquiring an asset, business or shares. The loan is normally secured on the asset or assets and the interest rate may be variable or fixed. The Small Firms Loan Guarantee Scheme can provide up to £250,000 of borrowing supported by a government guarantee where all other sources of finance have been exhausted.

### Mezzanino Debt

This is a loan finance where there is little or no security left after the senior debt has been secured. To reflect the higher risk of mezzanine funds, the lender will charge a rate of interest of perhaps four to eight per cent over bank base rate, may take an option to acquire some equity and may require repayment over a shorter term.

### Bank Overdraft

An overdraft is an agreed sum by which a customer can overdraw their current account. It is normally secured on current assets, repayable on demand and used for short term working capital fluctuations. The interest cost is normally variable and linked to bank base rate.

**Completing the finance-raising**

Raising finance is often a complex process. Business management need to assess several alternatives and then negotiate terms which are acceptable to the finance provider. The main negotiating points are often as follows:

- Whether equity investors take a seat on the board
- Votes ascribed to equity investors
- Level of warranties and indemnities provided by the directors
- Financier's fees and costs
- Who bears costs of due diligence.

During the finance-raising process, accountants are often called to review the financial aspects of the plan. Their report may be formal or informal, an overview or an extensive review of the company's management information system, forecasting methods and their accuracy, review of latest management accounts including working capital, pension funding and employee contracts etc. This due diligence process is used to highlight any fundamental problems that may exist.

## MANAGERIAL FINANCE

- What is Finance?
  - o Finance deals with decisions concerning cash inflows (financing) and cash outflows (investing); thus, nearly every decision made in the firm is somehow related to finance.
  - o *Everything else equal*, you should prefer (1) more value to less, (2) to receive cash sooner rather than later, and (3) less risk to more.

- General Areas of Finance
  - o Financial Markets and Institutions—the financial marketplace and the relationships of banking, insurance, estate planning, and so forth.
  - o Investments—evaluating financial assets, such as stocks and bonds, and determining which investments to include in a portfolio of financial assets.
  - o Financial Services—service organizations and mechanisms related to the management of money.
  - o Managerial Finance—often called corporate finance, includes decisions regarding types of real investments (i.e., plant and equipment) that should be made and how such investments should be financed (i.e., stocks or bonds), whether dividends should be paid, and so forth.
- The Importance of Finance in Nonfinance Areas—regardless of the area of business you study, an understanding of finance is crucial; decisions about money are commonplace in every area of business, thus financial decisions are required.
- Alternative Forms of Business Organization
  - o Proprietorship—single owner who is personally responsible for all liabilities of the firm; proprietorships represent about 70-75 percent of all businesses.

Advantages:

- easy and relatively inexpensive to form
- affected by few regulations
- business is taxed as an individual rather than a corporation

Disadvantages :

- owner has unlimited personal liability for debts of the firm
- firm's life is limited
- ownership transfer is similar to selling a house, which can be difficult
- firm's credit and its ability to raise funds is dependent on the financial strength of the owner
    - o Partnership—two or more owners who are personally responsible for all liabilities of the firm; advantages and disadvantages of a partnership are the same as for a proprietorship; partnerships represent about 8-10 percent of all businesses.
    - o Corporation—legal entity in which owners have limited responsibility for the liabilities of the firm; corporations represent about 20 percent of all businesses, but generate nearly 85 percent of all sales.

Advantages:

- unlimited life
- transfer of ownership is relatively simple—stock represents ownership
- limited liability of owners—generally limited to an investor's initial investment in the stock of the firm

Disadvantages:

- earnings are can be taxed twice, once at the corporate level and once when (if) distributed to stockholders as dividends
- establishing a corporation is more complex than for a proprietorship or a partnership

- Corporate charter—information about the corporation, including its name, type of business, amount of stock, and so forth.
- Bylaws—how the corporation will be governed

  o Hybrid Business Forms

Limited liability partnership (LLP)—a partnership where at least one partner is fully liable—the general partner—for the firms debts, but the liability of the other partners' generally is limited to the amount they invest in the business.

Limited liability corporation (LLC)—a business that offers limited liability to its owners like a regular corporation, but its income is taxed like a partnership; the structure of an LLC is very flexible with regard to ownership, governance, and so forth; unlike an S corporation, an LLC can have more than 100 stockholders and still be taxed like a partnership.

S Corporation—a corporation that has fewer than 100 stockholders can elect to be taxed as a partnership such that the income "passes through" to the stockholders and is not taxed at the corporate level.

- Primary Goal of the Corporation

  * Maximize wealth—should be the primary goal of the financial manager. Unlike profit (earnings per share, EPS) maximization, wealth maximization considers the impact of current decisions on the long-term financial health of the firm.
  * Social Responsibility—firms should be socially responsible at the same time they earn "normal" profits; otherwise they probably will go out of business.

* Wealth Maximization and Social Responsibility—actions that maximize the value of the firm also are beneficial to society; wealth maximization improves the standard of living.

- Shareholder Wealth Maximization—make decisions that maximize the current value of the cash flows that will be received in the future; the value of a firm can be computed as follows:

Decisions that affect cash flows affect the value of the firm. Financial decisions are based on the impact a behavior will have on the firm's expected future cash flows.

Such decisions include determining how to finance the firm (capital structure decisions), what assets to purchase (capital budgeting decisions), and whether to pay stockholders dividends or reinvest earnings in the firm (dividend policy decisions).

- Agency Relationships—persons who make decisions that affect the firm are "agents" who are responsible for acting in the best interests of the owners (stockholders) of the firm.

  o Agency problems arise when managers satisfy their own interests rather than the interests of the owners—that is, the common stockholders. Methods that help managers act in the best interests of owners include:

Managerial compensation (incentives)—reward managers for acting in the best interests of owners

Shareholder intervention—suggest remedies to problems, sponsor proposals/ changes to the governance of the firm, threaten to change the board of directors

Takeover threat—upper management generally is "let go" when a firm is taken over by another firm

  - o There is no agency problem/relationship in a proprietorship form of business, because the firm's owner also makes the firm's decisions; thus, he or she will make decisions that are in his or her best interest

- Business Ethics—"Standards of conduct or moral behavior"; "ethical" businesses "act" morally; generally "ethical" businesses are valued higher than similar business that are perceived to be unethical.
- Corporate Governance—how the firm is run/managed when doing business; the "rules" that the corporation follows when conducting business
- Forms of Business in Other Countries
  - o Foreign businesses are generally more closed than U.S. businesses—that is, foreign businesses are generally owned by fewer stockholders than U.S. businesses; ownership is more closely held
  - o Industrial groups—businesses in different industries that have common ownership; often the businesses complement each other—e.g., financing and marketing organizations might be aligned with manufacturers; in some cases suppliers, manufacturers, distributors, and retailers have common ownership.
- Multinational Corporations—firms that operate in more than one country
  - o Firms become more global to:

    seek new markets

    seek new sources of raw materials

    seek new technological advances

    seek more efficient production opportunities

avoid political and regulatory hurdles that apply to foreign manufacturers

o Factors that differentiate managerial finance in purely domestic firms and in multinational organizations include:

different currency denominations

economic and legal ramifications

language differences

cultural differences

government involvement

political risk

10

# RULES OF BUSINESS FINANCING

Business rules or business rulesets describe the operations, definitions and constraints that apply to an organization in achieving its goals. For example a business rule might state that no credit check is to be performed on return customers. Others could define a tenant in terms of solvency or list preferred suppliers and supply schedules. These rules are then used to help the organization to better achieve goals, communicate among principals and agents, communicate between the organization and interested third parties, demonstrate fulfillment of legal obligations, operate more efficiently, automate operations, perform analysis on current practices, etc.

## INTRODUCTION

Strategic management is distinct from business rules. Business rules are a means by which strategies are implemented. The rules tell an organization what it can do in detailed tactics, while the strategy tells it how to focus the business at a macro level to optimize results. Put differently, a strategy provides high-level direction about what an organization should do. Business rules can provide the tactical detail about exactly how a strategy will translate to actions. Example business rule domains include:

* marketing strategies
* pricing policies
* customer relationship management practices
* human resources activities
* regulatory forces, either to ensure compliance with regulations, or to make decisions under regulations (e.g. determining someone's tax bill or whether they are eligible for a government benefit)
* product and service offerings or operation workflows.

## HOW BUSINESS RULES ARE GATHERED

Business rules exist for an organization whether or not they are ever written down, talked about or even part of the organization's consciousness. However it is a fairly common practice for organizations to gather business rules in at least a very informal manner.

Organizations may choose to proactively describe their business practices in a database of rules. For example, they might hire a consultant to come through the organization to document and consolidate the various standards and methods currently in practice.

More commonly, business rules are discovered as part of a formal requirement gathering process during the initial stages of a project. In this case the collecting of the business rules are coincidental. Projects, such as the launching of a new product, might lead to a new body of business rules for an organization, i.e. this new product would require the employees to conceptualize about what the purpose of the organization is in a new way. This practice of coincidental business rule gathering is vulnerable to the creation of inconsistent or even conflicting business rules within different organizational units, or within the same organizational unit over time. Business Rules Methodology is the process of capturing business rules in English, in real-time while empowering users to manage rules with a few simple steps.

## REAL WORLD APPLICATIONS AND OBSTACLES

Despite many software vendors, consultants and research institutions offering business rules solutions, business rules are usually only gathered when dictated by law, as the first step in the automation process or as an ephemeral aid to engineers. This is mostly due to the overhead and effort required to maintain this database of rules. This becomes most severe the more dynamic and fluid the business rules for an organization are, for example in start-up companies. Another factor mitigating usage is the lack of incentive for employees to part with their most valuable asset to the organization; their knowledge of the business rules. A third factor is access to viable technology for maintaining business rules. A classic solution is the business rules engine. Rules engine products have been gaining traction in the market place.

Software packages automate business rules using business logic. The term business rule is sometimes used interchangeably with business logic; however the latter connotes an engineering practice and the former an intrinsic business practice. There is value in outlining an organization's business rules regardless of whether this information is used to automate its operations.

### Best Practices

1. *Declarative*: A business rule is a statement of truth about an organization. It is an attempt to describe the operations of an organization, not an attempt to prescribe how an organization should operate. This is why business rules are said to be discovered or observed and not created.

2. *Atomic*: A rule is either completely true or completely false; there are no shades of gray. For example a rule for an airline that states passengers may upgrade to first class round-trip tickets if seats are available and they pay the fare increase does not imply that this deal is available for just one leg of the journey.
3. *Distinct, independent constructs*: Separate the things that define your business (the rules) from the processes (i.e. strategies and tactics). Don't build complex and cyclical dependencies-simplify and flatten the constructs.
4. *Expressed in natural language*: In order to appeal to the broadest audience, it is almost always best to express business rules in a natural language without the use of a lot of technical jargon.
5. *Business, not technology, oriented*: For example, a company's business rules should not be foreign to a knowledgeable customer.
6. *Business, not technology, owned*: Business rules come from business decisions. These are independent from implementation decisions.

## Formal Specification

Business rules can be expressed in a very formal language. An example of when this rigour is required is in highly technical enterprises such as the building of a bridge. Another example is a project trying to automate the business rules gathering process.

Example languages include Unified Modeling Language, Z notation, Business Process Execution Language, Web Services Policy Framework, Business Process Modeling Notation, or Semantics of Business Vocabulary and Business Rules (SBVR).

## BUSINESS MODEL

The term business model describes a broad range of informal and formal models that are used by enterprises to represent various aspects of business, such as operational processes, organizational structures, and financial forecasts. Although the term can be traced to the 1950s, it achieved mainstream usage only in the 1990s. Many informal definitions of the term can be found in popular business literature, such as the following:

> *"A business model is a conceptual tool that contains a big set of elements and their relationships and allows expressing the business logic of a specific firm. It is a description of the value a company offers to one or several segments of customers and of the architecture of the firm and its network of partners for creating, marketing, and delivering this value and relationship capital, to generate profitable and sustainable revenue streams"-Osterwalder, Pigneur and Tucci (2005)*

More recently, researchers build definitions based on economic and organizational theories and show that the definitions are econometrically sound. For example, Malone, et al. (2006) at MIT propose an operational definition of business model, based on theories such as those from transaction cost economics. Zott and Amit (2002) from INSEAD and Wharton based their definition on boundary-spanning transactions.

Simply put: What problem does this business solve and how does it do so profitably?

## COMPONENTS OF A BUSINESS MODEL

Many different conceptualizations of business models exist (Chesbrough and Rosenbloom 2000; Hamell 2000; Linder and Cantrell 2000; Petrovic, Kittl et al.; Weill and Vitale 2001; Gordijn 2002; Afuah and Tucci 2003;

Osterwalder 2004; Fetscherin & Knolmayer 2005). They all have various degrees of resemblance or difference.

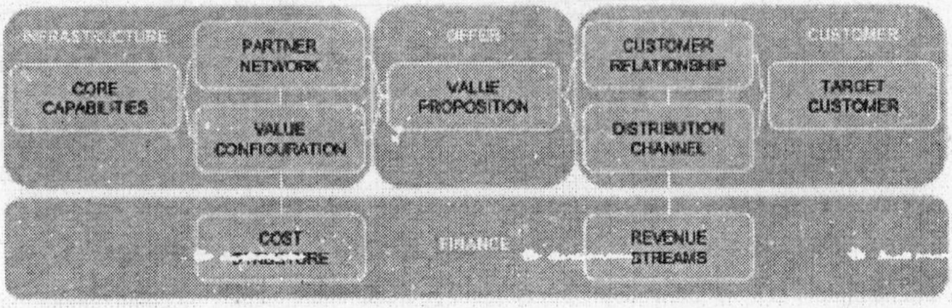


The model proposed by Osterwalder (2004) synthesises the different conceptualizations into a single reference model based on the similarities of a large range of models. The author's conceptualization describes a business model as consisting of nine related business model building blocks. Thus, a business model describes a company's business:

### *Infrastructure*

- *Core capabilities*: The capabilities and competencies necessary to execute a company's business model.
- *Partner network*: The business alliances which complement other aspects of the business model.
- *Value configuration*: The rationale which makes a business mutually beneficial for a business and its customers.

### *Offering*

- *Value proposition*: The products and services a business offers.

### *Customers*

- *Target customer*: The target audience for a business' products and services.
- *Distribution channel*: The means by which a company delivers products and services to customers. This

includes the company's marketing and distribution strategy.

- *Customer relationship*: The links a company establishes between itself and its different customer segments. The process of managing customer relationships is referred to as customer relationship management.

***Finances***

- *Cost structure*: The monetary consequences of the means emplcyed in the business model. A company's DOC.
- *Revenue*: The way a company makes money through a variety of revenue flows. A company's income.

These 9 business model building blocks constitute a business model design template which allows companies to describe their business model.

**Evolution**

A brief history of the development of business models might run as follows. The oldest and most basic business model is the shop keeper model. This involves setting up a store in a location where potential customers are likely to be and displaying a product or service.

Over the years, business models have become much more sophisticated. The bait and hook business model (also referred to as the "razor and blades business model" or the "tied products business model") was introduced in the early 20th century. This involves offering a basic product at a very low cost, often at a loss (the "bait"), then charging compensatory recurring amounts for refills or associated products or services (the "hook"). Examples include: razor (bait) and blades (hook); cell phones (bait) and air time (hook); computer printers (bait) and ink cartridge refills (hook); and cameras (bait) and prints (hook). An interesting variant of this model is a software developer that gives away its word processor reader for free but charges several hundred dollars for its word processor writer.

In the 1950s, new business models came from McDonald's Restaurants and Toyota. In the 1960s, the innovators were Wal-Mart and Hypermarkets. The 1970s saw new business models from FedEx and Toys R Us; the 1980s from Blockbuster, Home Depot, Intel, and Dell Computer; the 1990s from Southwest Airlines, Netflix, eBay, Amazon.com, and Starbucks. Poorly thought out business models were a problem with many dot-coms.

Today, the type of business models might depend on how technology is used. For example, entrepreneurs on the internet have also created entirely new models that depend entirely on existing or emergent technology. Using technology, businesses can reach a large number of customers with minimal costs.

### Example Business Models over the Years

- The open business model
- The subscription business model
- The razor and blades business model (bait and hook)
- The pyramid scheme business model
- The multi-level marketing business model
- The network effects business model
- The monopolistic business model
- The cutting out the middleman model
- The auction business model
- The online auction business model
- The bricks and clicks business model

- The loyalty business models
- The Collective business models
- The industrialization of services business model
- The servitization of products business model
- The low-cost carrier business model
- The online content business model
- The freemium business model
- The premium business model
- The direct sales model
- The professional open-source model
- Various distribution business models

**Do Business Models Matter?**

Malone et al. (2006) at MIT find that some business models, as defined by them, indeed performed better than others in a dataset consisting of the largest U.S. firms, in the period 1998 through 2002.

Zott and Amit (2002) also link business models to performance, in the context of 190 young, growth-oriented firms in the US and Europe that had gone public between 1996 and 2000. See also their additional research on value drivers.

Business Model Innovation has become increasingly important as the recent IBM CEO survey 2006 shows. See also a video resource by Osterwalder (2006) on what the implications of business model innovation are and how it can be achieved.

**Related Concepts**

The process of business model design is part of business strategy. The implementation of a company's business model into organizational structures (e.g. organigrams, workflows, human resources) and systems (e.g. information technology architecture, production lines) is part of a company's business operations.

It is important to understand that business modeling commonly refers to business process design at the operational level, whereas business models and business model design refer to defining the business logic of a company at the strategic level.

## BUSINESS MODEL DESIGN

Business model design refers to the activity of designing a company's business model. It is part of the business development and business strategy process and involves design methods. Business model design includes the modeling and description of a company's:

- value propositions
- target customer segments
- distribution channels
- customer relationships
- value configurations
- core capabilities
- partner network
- cost structure
- revenue model

Business model design is distinct from business modeling. The former refers to defining the business logic of a company at the strategic level, whereas the latter refers to business process design at the operational level. A business model design template can facilitate the process of designing and describing a company's business model.

## BUSINESS PLAN

This is a summary article that covers many topics related to business plans-their content, how they are used, legal issues, and spoofs of business plans, among others.-please see individual sections for links to detailed discussions of various topics relating to business plans.

A business plan is a formal statement of a set of business goals, the reasons why they are believed attainable, and the plan for reaching those goals. It may also contain background information about the organization or team attempting to reach those goals.

The business goals being attempted may be for-profit or non-profit. For-profit business plans typically focus on financial goals. Non-profit and government agency business plans tend to focus on service goals. Business plans may also target changes in perception and branding by the customer, client, tax-payer, or larger community. A business plan that has changes in perception and branding as its primary goals is called a marketing plan.

Business plans may be internally or externally focused. Externally focused plans target goals that are important to external stakeholders, particularly financial stakeholders. They typically have detailed information about the organization or team attempting to reach the goals. With for-profit entities, external stakeholders include investors and customers. External stake-holders of non-profits include donors and the clients of the non-profit's services. For government agencies, external stakeholders include tax-payers, higher-level government agencies, and international lending bodies such as the IMF, the World Bank, various economic agencies of the UN, and development banks.

Internally focused business plans target intermediate goals required to reach the external goals. They may cover the development of a new product, a new service, a new IT system, a restructuring of finance, the refurbishing of a factory or a restructuring of the organization. An internal business is often developed in conjunction with a balanced scorecard or a list of critical success factors. This allows success of the plan to be measured using non-financial measures. Business plans that identify and target internal goals, but provide only general guidance on how they will be met are called strategic plans.

Operational plans describe the goals of an internal organization, working group or department. Project plans, sometimes known as project frameworks, describe the goals of a particular project. They may also address the project's place within the organization's larger strategic goals.

**Business Plan Content**

Business plans are decision making tools. There is no fixed content for a business plan. Rather the content and format of the business plan is determined by the goals and audience. A business plan should contain whatever information is needed to decide whether or not to pursue a goal.

For example, a business plan for a non-profit might discuss the fit between the business plan and the organization's mission. Banks are quite concerned about defaults, so a business plan for a bank loan will build a convincing case for the organization's ability to repay the loan. Venture capitalists are primarily concerned about initial investment, feasibility, and exit valuation. A business plan for a project requiring equity financing will need to explain why current resources, upcoming growth opportunities, and sustainable competitive advantage will lead to a high exit valuation.

Preparing a business plan draws on a wide range of knowledge from many different business disciplines: finance, human resource management, intellectual property management, supply chain management, operations management, and marketing, among others. . It can be helpful to view the business plan as a collection of sub-plans, one for each of the main business disciplines.

### Business Plan Preparation

### Support Services

- books, portals, and other sources of written information
- consultancies
- electronic planning templates (software)
- face to face help: mentoring programs, training courses
  - — USA: SCORE, SBA centers
  - — Morocco: CRI (Centre Régional d'Investisiment)
  - — England: Business Link
  - — Pakistan: SMEDA (Small and medium enterprise development authority)
  - — Other countries: needs research

## RESOURCES FOR RESEARCHING FACTS AND FIGURES

### Internal Corporate Records

#### *Free Information*

- published statistics on the web
- free articles and abstracts from consulting firms
- alumni resources-many undergraduate and graduate programs provide access to library and/or campus business center services as part of their package of alumni services.

### *Fee-based Services*

- marketing reports from subscription services
- archive and journal services
- books

### *Strategic Analysis*

- Industry Assessment
  - — The macroenvironment
  - — Customer Strategy & Market Analysis
- Competitor Analysis
  - — Porter 5 forces analysis

## Forecasts: Modeling Techniques

### *Presentation Formats*

The format of a business plan depends on its presentation context. It is not uncommon for businesses, especially start-ups to have three or four formats for the same business plan:

- an "elevator pitch"-a three minute summary of the business plan's executive summary. This is often used as a teaser to awaken the interest of potential funders, customers, or strategic partners.
- an oral presentation-a hopefully entertaining slide show and oral narrative that is meant to trigger discussion and interest potential investors in reading the written presentation. The content of the presentation is usually limited to the executive summary and a few key graphs showing financial trends and key decision making benchmarks. If a new product is being proposed and time permits, a demonstration of the product may also be included.

- a written presentation for external stakeholders-a detailed, well written, and pleasingly formatted plan targeted at external stakeholders.
- an internal operational plan-a detailed plan describing planning details that are needed by management but may not be of interest to external stakeholders. Such plans have a somewhat higher degree of candor and informality than the version targeted at external stakeholders.

## Revisiting the Business Plan

### *Cost Overruns and Revenue Shortfalls*

Cost and revenue estimates are central to any business plan for deciding the viability of the planned venture. But costs are often underestimated and revenues overestimated resulting in later cost overruns, revenue shortfalls, and possibly non-viability. During the dot-com bubble 1997-2001 this was a problem for many technology start-ups. However, the problem is not limited to technology or the private sector; public works projects also routinely suffer from cost overruns and/or revenue shortfalls. The main causes of cost overruns and revenue shortfalls are optimism bias and strategic misrepresentation.

## Legal and Liability Issues

### *Disclosure Requirements*

An externally targeted business plan should list all legal concerns and financial liabilities that might negatively affect investors. Depending on the amount of funds being raised and the audience to whom the plan is presented, failure to do this may have severe legal consequences.

## Limitations on Content and Audience

Non disclosure agreements (NDAs) with third parties, non-compete agreements, conflicts of interest, privacy concerns, and the protection of one's trade secrets may severely limit the audience to which one might show the business plan. Alternatively, they may require each party receiving the business plan to sign a contract accepting special clauses and conditions.

This situation is complicated by the fact that many venture capitalists will refuse to sign an NDA before looking at a business plan, lest it put them in the untenable position of looking at two independently developed look-alike business plans, both claiming originality. In such situations one may need to develop two versions of the business plan: a stripped down plan that can be used to develop a relationship and a detail plan that is only shown when investors have sufficient interest and trust to sign an NDA.

## How Business Plans are Used

### *Venture Capital*

- business plan contests-provides a way for venture capitals to find promising projects
- venture capital assessment of business plans-focus on qualitative factors such as team.

## Education

### *K-12*

Business plans are used in some primary and secondary programs to teach economic principles.

Wikiversity has a v:Lunar Boom Town project where students of all ages can collaborate with designing and revising business models and practice evaluating them to learn practical business planning techniques and methodology.

### *Higher Education*

- BA, MBA programs

— integrative team projects

— projects for specific course work

— Business plan contests

## Satires of Business Plans

The business plan is the subject of many satires. Satires are used both to express cynicism about business plans and as an educational tool to improve the quality of business plans. For example,

- Five Criteria for a successful business plan in biotech uses Dilbert comic strips to remind people of what not to do when researching and writing a business plan for a biotech start-up. Scott Adams, the author of Dilbert, is an MBA graduate (U.C. Berkeley) who sees humor as a critical tool that can improve the behavior of businesses and their managers. He has written numerous critiques of business practices, including business planning. The website Dilbert.com-Games has a mission statement generator that satires the wording often found in mission statements. His book The Dilbert Principle-A Cubicle's Eye View of Bosses, Meetings, Management Fads & Other Workplace Afflictions discusses the foibles of management and their plans as depicted in the Dilbert comic strips by Scott Adams.
- In the article "South Park's" Investing Lesson, the The Motley Fool columnist "Fool on the Hill" uses the Underpants Gnomes to illustrate the fallacy of focusing on goals without a clear implementation strategy. The Underpants Gnomes episode satires the business plans of the Dot.com era. It features a three-part business plan for a new coffee shop:

  1. Collect underpants
  2. Profit!

# BIBLIOGRAPHY


Adelberg, Edward A.: *Papers on Bacterial Genetics*, Boston, Brown and Company, 1960.

Angel, Bradley: *Toxic Threat to Indian Lands: A Greenpeace Report*, San Francisco, Greenpeace, 1991.

Baker, S. H.: *Character Building Clubs for Boys. The Scientific Management of Clubs for Boys*, London, YMCA Boys Department, 1919.

Barnum, Susan R.: *Biotechnology: An Introduction*, Belmont, Thomson/Brooks/Cole, 2005.

Burch, William R. Jr.: *Human Ecology: An Environmental Approach*, Belmont, Duxbury Press, 1994.

Campbell, R. R., and Wade, J. L.: *Society and Environment: The Coming Collision*, Boston, Allyn and Bacon, 1972.

Carey, W.: *Public Opinion and the Communication of Consent*, New York: Guilford Publications, 1995.

Chrispeels, Maarten : *Plants, Genes and Crop Biotechnology*, Sudbury MA, Jones and Barlett Publishers, 2003.

Cox, Earl D. : *Beyond Humanity: Cyber Evolution and Future Minds*, Roackland, Charles River Media, 1996.

Daubenmire, R. F.: *Plants and Environment*, New York, Wiley, 1947.

David Sadava: *Plants, Genes and Crop Biotechnology*, Sudbury MA, Jones and Barlett Publishers, 2003.

Dixon, Dougal: *After Man-A Zoology of the Future*, New York, St. Martin's Press, 1981.

Dodds, John H.: *Plant Genetic Engineering*, New York, Cambridge University Press, 1985.

Edwards-Rees, D.: *The Service of Youth Book*, Wallington, Religious Education Press, 1943.

Gitman, Lawrence J.: *Principles of Managerial Finance*, MA: Addison Wesley Longman, 2000.

Hill, David: *The Quality of Life in America; Pollution, Poverty, Power, and Fear*, New York, Holt, Rinehart and Winston, 1973.

Johnson, Hazel: *Financial Institutions and Markets: A Global Perspective*, NY, McGraw Hill, 1993.

Kruvant, W.J.: *People, Energy, and Pollution*, Cambridge, Ballinger Publishing, 1975.

Martin, Justin: *The Man Behind Money*, Perseus Book Group, 2000.

Matthews, J. E.: *Working with Youth Groups*, London, University of London Press, 1966.

Milson, F.: *Growing With the Job*, London, National Assocation of Youth Clubs, 1968.

Petty, Keown, Scott, and Martin: *Basic Financial Management*, Prentice Hall, 1993.

Primrose, S.B.: *Principles of Gene Manipulation*, London, Blackwell Scientific Publications, 1989.

Rifkin, Jeremy: *The Biotech Century*, New York, Penguin Putnam, 1998

Schall and Haley: *Introduction to Financial Management*, McGraw-hill, 1988.

Vallette, J.: *The International Trade in Wastes: A Greenpeace Inventory*, Washington, Greenpeace, 1989.

Walden, Richard: *Genetic Transformation in Plants*, England, Open University Press, 1988.

Zupan, J.M.: *The Distribution of Air Quality in the New York Region*, Baltimore, Johns Hopkins University Press, 1973.

# INDEX